Let There Be Light

A Healthy Cookbook
from

CHRISTUS
Health

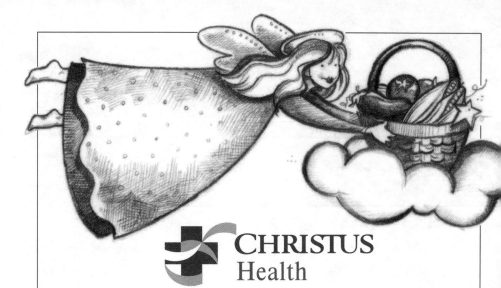

CHRISTUS
Health

6363 N. Highway 161, Suite 450
Irving, TX 75038

CHRISTUS Health is a not-for-profit health care system that
includes more than 40 hospitals and other health care ministries
in more than 70 communities in Texas, Louisiana, Arkansas,
Utah, Oklahoma and Mexico.

It is the Mission of CHRISTUS Health
to extend the healing ministry of Jesus Christ.

Proceeds from this cookbook will benefit CHRISTUS Health Ministries.

©Copyright 2001, CHRISTUS Health LCCN: 200118626
ISBN: 0-9714055-0-6 First Printing, 12,000 copies, November 2001.
Printed in the United States of America
TOOF COOKBOOK DIVISION

STARR★TOOF

670 South Cooper St., Memphis, TN 38104

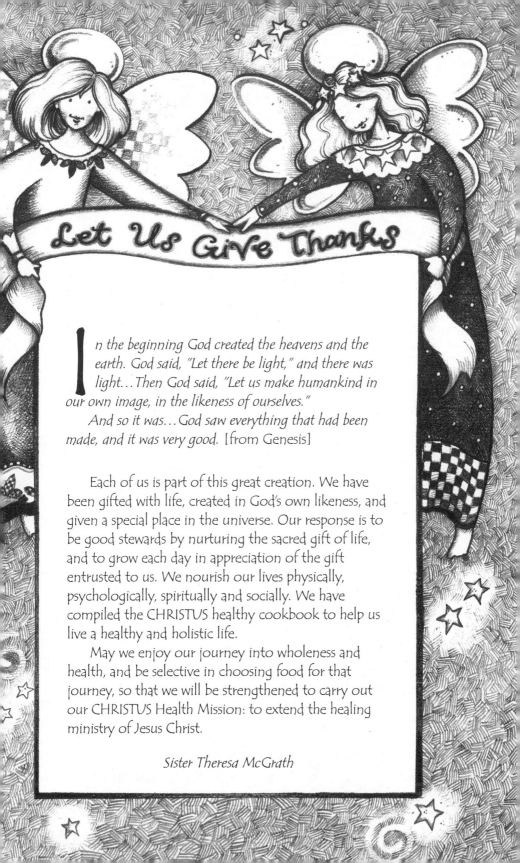

Let Us Give Thanks

In the beginning God created the heavens and the earth. God said, "Let there be light," and there was light…Then God said, "Let us make humankind in our own image, in the likeness of ourselves."

And so it was…God saw everything that had been made, and it was very good. [from Genesis]

Each of us is part of this great creation. We have been gifted with life, created in God's own likeness, and given a special place in the universe. Our response is to be good stewards by nurturing the sacred gift of life, and to grow each day in appreciation of the gift entrusted to us. We nourish our lives physically, psychologically, spiritually and socially. We have compiled the CHRISTUS healthy cookbook to help us live a healthy and holistic life.

May we enjoy our journey into wholeness and health, and be selective in choosing food for that journey, so that we will be strengthened to carry out our CHRISTUS Health Mission: to extend the healing ministry of Jesus Christ.

Sister Theresa McGrath

In Appreciation

CHRISTUS Health would like to thank the following individuals and organizations that contributed to this cookbook:

CHRISTUS St. Joseph Hospital Volunteers

CHRISTUS Spohn Auxiliary Association

CHRISTUS St. Catherine Hospital Volunteers

CHRISTUS Schumpert Radiology and Pathology Associates

CHRISTUS Santa Rosa Registered Dieticians

The American Heart Association

The Juvenile Diabetes Foundation

The Diabetes Research Foundation

CHRISTUS Health Communications Council

Linda McClung, Sr. Vice President, Communications & Public Affairs

Heather Boler, Director Marketing & Communications

Christie Galvin, Director Public Affairs

Molly Beekley Communications Specialist Text & Editing

Mark Hopkins Communications Specialist

Patricia Ward Communications Assistant Production

Melissa Martinez, Receptionist Production

Alice Buske, Office Manager Production

Arnetta Autrey, Exccecutive Assistant

Joyce LeMay Production

Meet the Artist

Dana Stewart is a gifted artist and designer who has a special way with angels. She lives in Webster Groves, Missouri with her own little angels, Hally and Maddy, her husband, Larry, and two spoiled cats that rule the house!

Contents

One of the most wonderful things about the human body is its amazing ability to heal itself. Over the past five years, scientists have compiled a wealth of data about what happens when we change our eating and exercise habits. They have found that even fairly small changes can make a huge difference in our health...that as much as 70% of all chronic diseases in the U.S., including diabetes and high blood pressure, heart disease and some cancers, can be avoided with a few sensible lifestyle changes.

Did you know?

- ❖ Eating more fruits, vegetables and fiber changes our blood's sensitivity to insulin within a few weeks, helping to decrease your diabetes risk very quickly.

- ❖ Women who eat just eight ounces of fish a week can cut their risk of stroke by almost half.

- ❖ A brisk, half-hour walk four days a week can lower a person's risk of heart attack to almost the same level as a person who has exercised all her life.

- ❖ A smoker who quits for five years will lower his or her risk of heart attack to almost the same level as one who has never smoked.

- ❖ Not all fats are bad for you...some fats are good for you!

- ❖ Researchers have found that five servings of vegetables and fruits per day can lower your risk of cancer, cardiovascular disease, and other chronic diseases. Vegetables and fruits are important sources of essential nutrients and fiber that protect us from common diseases.

Applesauce Cinnamon Muffins

1¼	c. oat bran cereal, uncooked	¾	c. unsweetened applesauce
1	c. whole wheat flour	½	c. honey
2	tsp. ground cinnamon	½	c. vegetable oil
1	T. baking powder	1	egg
¾	tsp. baking soda	1	T. pure vanilla extract
½	tsp. salt	¼	c. walnuts (optional)

Coat 12 muffin cups with vegetable oil or line with baking cups. In medium bowl, combine oat bran cereal, flour, cinnamon, baking powder, soda and salt. In a large bowl, combine applesauce, honey, oil, egg and vanilla. Stir in dry ingredients and mix well. Stir in nuts. Fill muffin cups almost full. Bake in a 375-degree oven 15-20 minutes, or until golden. Makes 1 dozen. Each muffin, 23g. cholesterol, 3g protein, 7 g. fat, 159 calories. Exchanges: 1 starch/bread + 1 fat exchange + 1 fruit exchange.
Miles Johnson

Peanut Butter Bran Muffins

½	c. whole-wheat flour	1	egg
⅓	c. bran	¼	c. peanut butter
2	tsp. baking powder	½	c. lowfat milk
1	T. sugar	⅓	c. peanuts, chopped

Combine flour, bran, baking powder and sugar in a bowl. Add the remaining ingredients and blend. Spoon into oiled muffin tin or paper muffin cups. Bake in a 375-degree oven for 15-20 minutes. Makes 8, each 140 calories, 12g carbohydrates, 6g protein, 9g sodium. Exchanges: 1 bread, 2 fat.
Janet Young

To eat is human; to digest divine. *Mark Twain*

Mom's Pretzels

1	pkg. active dry yeast	4	c. flour, unbleached
1¹/₂	c. warm water	1	lg. egg, beaten
1	tsp. salt		coarse salt (optional)
1	T. sugar		

Dissolve yeast in warm water. Add salt and sugar to yeast mixture. Blend in flour and knead dough until smooth, about 8 minutes. Cover and allow dough to rise until it is double in size. Punch down. Cut dough into small pieces and roll into "ropes." Twist pieces into pretzel shapes and place on a greased cookie sheet. Brush pretzels with egg using a pastry brush. Sprinkle with coarse salt. Allow dough to rise again until almost double in bulk. Bake at 425 degrees for 10 to 15 minutes, or until golden brown. Makes 12, each 25 calories.
Becky Henderson

Irish Soda Bread

3	c. flour	¹/₂	tsp. salt
¹/₃	c. sugar	1	egg
2	T. butter	1	c. low-fat milk
1	tsp. baking soda		raisins and caraway seeds
3	tsp. baking powder		(optional – to taste)

Melt butter. Add flour and sugar and mix together. Add baking soda, baking powder and salt, and mix again. Add raisins and caraway seeds according to taste. Beat egg. Add cup of milk to egg and beat together. Add egg/milk mixture to dry ingredients, a little at a time, until the mixture is stiff and sticky. Butter and flour the bottom of an 8" round cake pan. Put mixture in pan, sprinkling a little flour on top so you can spread the dough. Use a fork to poke holes across the top of the dough. Bake in a 375-degree oven 45-50 minutes, or until light brown. Cool and slice. Great with jam! Each slice, 35 calories.
Evelyn Smith

Mexican Cornbread

1¹/₂	c. cornmeal	2	eggs
1	c. sour cream	1	medium green pepper, chopped
1	c. canned cream-style corn		
²/₃	c. vegetable oil	1	jalapeno, chopped
3	tsp. baking powder	2	c. cheddar cheese, shredded
1	tsp. salt		

Mix together all ingredients except cheese. Pour half of the mixture into a well-greased hot skillet. Sprinkle half of the cheese on top. Repeat layers. Bake at 350 for 35 to 40 minutes. Exchange: 1 bread, 1 fat, ¹/₂ high-fat meat.
Kathleen Childs

Burst o'Lemon Muffins

1³/₄	c. all-purpose flour
³/₄	c. sugar
1	tsp. baking powder
³/₄	t. baking soda
¹/₄	tsp. sale
1	c. lemon or vanilla yogurt
1	egg
¹/₃	c. butter or margarine, melted
1	T. lemon juice
1 to 2 T. grated lemon peel	
¹/₂	c. flaked coconut (optional)

Topping

¹/₃	c. lemon juice
¹/₄	c. sugar
¹/₄	c. flaked coconut, toasted

In a large bowl, combine flour, sugar, baking powder, baking soda and salt. In another bowl, beat the yogurt, egg, butter, lemon peel and juice until smooth. Stir the wet mixture into the dry ingredients until just moistened. Fold in coconut. Fill greased muffin cups ²/₃ full. Bake at 400 degrees for 18-20 minutes before removing from pan to wire rack.

To make topping, combine lemon juice and sugar in a saucepan. Cook and stir until sugar is dissolved. Stir in coconut. Poke 6-8 holes in each muffin with a toothpick. Spoon coconut mixture over muffins. Makes 1 dozen. Exchange: 1 bread, 1 fat.
Pat Walker

Applesauce Raisin Bread

1¹/₂	c. flour	1	c. brown sugar (firmly packed)
3	tsp. baking powder	2	eggs
1	tsp. salt	¹/₃	c. vegetable oil
1	tsp. cinnamon	1	c. applesauce
¹/₂	tsp. nutmeg	1	c. raisins
1	c. quick oats	¹/₂	c. nuts, chopped

Combine dry ingredients. Add eggs, oil and applesauce. Stir until well mixed. Stir in raisins and nuts. Pour into greased 9x5x3 inch loaf pan. Bake at 350 degrees for 1 hour. Exchange: 1 bread, ¹/₂ fat, ¹/₂ fruit.
Helene Murphy

Tangy Guacamole

2	large ripe avocados, peeled, pitted and mashed	1	T. fresh lime juice
			Tortilla chips
¹/₃	c. thick and chunky salsa		
1	clove garlic, crushed and minced		

Mix avocado, salsa, garlic and lime juice in a bowl. Serve with tortilla chips. Makes 2 cups. Calories per tablespoon (without chips), 20; fat, 2 g; cholesterol, 0 mg.
Molly Beekley

Make it light! Try dipping with baked or fat-free chips; use as a topping for baked potato skins, packed with nutrients.

What hymns are sung, what praises said
for homemade miracles of bread? *Louis Untermeyer*

Tuna Stuffed Jalapenos

24 jalapenos, canned
1 8-oz. can tuna fish in water, drained
1 16-oz. container soft cream cheese

Cut jalapenos lengthwise in half and remove seeds. Cream together cream cheese and tuna until smooth. Stuff jalapeno halves. Refrigerate until time to serve. Makes 48. Calories per 2-piece serving, 25; fat, 3 g.
Rhoda Cavin

Make it light! Use fat-free cream cheese to eliminate fat grams.

Artichoke Dip

2 8-oz. cans artichoke hearts, drained
1 small jar marinated artichoke hearts with liquid
1 8-oz. can green chili sauce
2 8-oz. cans chopped chilies
8 oz. Monterey jack cheese with jalapenos, shredded

Chop artichokes in food processor. In large mixing bowl, combine remaining ingredients. Add artichokes. Spread in baking dish and bake at 350 for 30 minutes. Serve with crackers.
Rose M. Yawn

Make it light! Use low-fat cheese to save fat and calories.

May two angels guard my bed,
One at the foot and one at the head.

Sausage Balls

16	oz. turkey breakfast sausage	2	eggs
6	T. Parmesan cheese, grated	1/2	tsp. ground pepper
2	slices light bread, crumbled	1/4	c. finely diced celery
2	T. dried parsley flakes	1/4	c. finely diced onions

Mix all ingredients until well blended. Form into individual balls, approximately 1/2 tablespoon each. Place balls on cookie sheet that has been coated with non-stick cooking spray. To cook, place balls in 350-degree oven for 12 minutes, or until brown. Makes 40.
2 sausage balls = 1 meat exchange, 2 g fat, 1 g carbohydrate, 21 mg cholesterol, 36 mg sodium.
Becky Waggoner

Shrimp Ceviche

2	lbs. shrimp, boiled and peeled	1	small purple onion, thinly sliced
	juice of 6 lemons	1	jalapeno, diced
	juice of 3 limes or sour oranges		cilantro to taste, chopped

Place cooled shrimp in a glass or ceramic bowl and cover with citrus juices, onion, jalapeno and cilantro. Add salt and pepper to taste. Refrigerate 4 to 6 hours. Serving suggestion: arrange on a bed of lettuce with pieces of cooked sweet potato and chunks of corn on the cob. Serves 8, each 2 meat, 1/2 fruit, 1/2 vegetable.
Amy Walsh

A bagel is a doughnut with the sin removed.
George Rosenbaum

Texas Shrimp Dip

1	c. shrimp, cooked, peeled and chopped	1/4	c. mayonnaise
8	oz. cream cheese, softened	1/4	tsp. salt
1	small onion, chopped	1/4	tsp. white pepper

Combine ingredients and garnish as desired. Serve with crackers. Six fat grams per tablespoon.
Kathleen Childs

Make it light! Substitute fat-free or low-fat cream cheese and mayonnaise to cut out the fat.

Spinach Dip

1	10-oz. pkg. frozen chopped spinach, thawed and drained	1	pkg. (1.4 oz.) vegetable soup mix
1 1/2	c. sour cream	1	can (8 oz.) water chestnuts, drained and chopped
1	c. mayonnaise	3	green onions, chopped

In medium bowl, combine spinach, sour cream, mayonnaise, soup mix, water chestnuts and green onions. Cover and chill. Serve with fresh vegetables, crackers or chips. Nine fat grams per tablespoon.
Aynne Daugherty, R.N.

Make it light! Use low-fat versions of sour cream and mayonnaise for a guilt-free snack.

Low-Fat, Spicy Buffalo "Wings"

2	T. hot sauce, or to taste	
	Pinch cayenne	
1/4	tsp. Paprika	
1/2	lb. chicken breast tenders	
	celery sticks	

Dressing

1/2	c. reduced-fat blue cheese dressing
1/4	c. fat-free mayonnaise
3	T. crumbled blue cheese

In a medium bowl, combine hot sauce, cayenne and paprika. Add chicken tenders to coat. Place chicken tenders on a nonstick baking sheet and bake at 375 degrees for 15 minutes, or until tender. Combine dressing ingredients and serve alongside the chicken with celery sticks. Serves 4, each 4 g fat.
Kimberly Francis

Seafood Cocktail Sauce

3/4	c. ketchup		1/2	green pepper, seeded and diced
1/2	c. chili sauce			
1	T. horseradish, or to taste		1	tsp. Finely chopped celery
2	tsp. Worcestershire sauce			

Combine all ingredients and mix well. Chill at least one hour before serving. Makes 1/2 cup of sauce for shrimp, crab, lobster or your favorite seafood. Exchange: free per 2 T. serving.
Tommy Joyce Pinkston

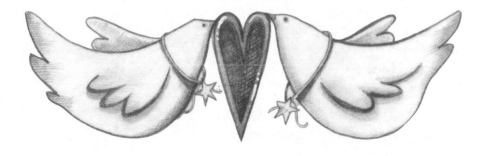

Asparagus Bundles

48	thin asparagus spears	1	T. water
2½	ounces soft fresh goat cheese	1	tsp. grated orange peel
	(such as Montrachet), room	2	oz. thinly sliced prosciutto
	temperature		(Italian ham), cut into
	2 T. chopped fresh basil		twenty-four 4 x 1-inch strips
1	T. toasted pine nuts, chopped		

Cut stalks from asparagus, leaving 2-inch-long tips. (Reserve asparagus stalks for a salad or pasta dish.) Cook asparagus tips in large pot of boiling salted water until just crisp-tender, about 1 minute. Drain. Transfer asparagus to paper towels and drain well. Mix goat cheese, basil, pine nuts, water and orange peel in small bowl to blend. Season with salt and pepper. Spread scant 1 teaspoon filling over each prosciutto strip. Arrange 2 asparagus tips atop filling at 1 short end of prosciutto. Roll up prosciutto, enclosing base of asparagus. Press to seal. Place on platter. (Can be made 1 day ahead. Cover; chill.) Serves 6, each 78 calories.
Patricia Ward

Hot Reuben Dip

1	8-oz. pkg. dream cheese, softened	4	oz. deli sliced corned beef, chopped
1½	c. Swiss cheese, shredded	½	c. sauerkraut, drained
½	c. Thousand Island dressing		

Mix cream cheese, one cup of the Swiss cheese, the dressing and corned beef. Spread in a 9-inch pie plate. Top with sauerkraut and remaining Swiss cheese. Bake at 400 degrees for about 15 minutes, or until bubbly. Serve hot with cocktail rye bread. Makes 2½ cups. Calories per ¼ cup: 220, fat, 18 g; cholesterol, 55 mg; sodium, 820 mg.
Reba Darby

Make it light! Use low-fat cream cheese, Swiss cheese and salad dressing to cut fat grams. For every fat gram saved, you save 9 calories!

Corn and Olive Spread

2	8-oz. pkg. cream cheese, softened	1	can (14-1/4 oz.) ripe olives, drained and chopped
1	1-oz. pkg. dry ranch-style dressing mix	1	can (11 oz.) whole kernel corn, drained
1	medium red bell pepper, chopped		

Beat cream cheese and dressing mix in large bowl until smooth. Stir in remaining ingredients. Cover and refrigerate at least one hour to blend flavors. Serve with crackers or tortilla chips. Makes about 4 cups. Calories, per tablespoon, 35; fat, 3 g; cholesterol, 10 mg; sodium, 100 mg.; carbohydrate, 1 g.
Mary Valle Cooper

Make it light! Fat-free cream cheese will reduce the calories to 8 and the fat grams to one!

Tomato Aspic

1	T. unflavored gelatin	2	c. Bloody Mary mix
2	T. cold water	1	pkg. lemon gelatin
2	T. boiling water		Green pepper and celery, chopped, for garnish
1	can condensed tomato soup		

Soak gelatin in cold water. Dissolve in boiling water. Add tomato soup and stir. Heat Bloody Mary mix and dissolve lemon gelatin in the hot liquid. Slowly combine two mixtures. Chill until firm. Garnish with celery and green pepper. 0 fat grams.
Peggy Smith

A world without tomatoes is like a string quartet without violins. *Laurie Colwin*

Refreshing Cranberry Tea

2   c. cold brewed tea
2   c. chilled cranberry or cran-
     raspberry juice

2   c. chilled sparkling water
     Fresh mint leaves
     Fresh raspberries

Mix all liquids together and serve over ice. Garnish with fresh mint and raspberries. Makes 6 servings. Per serving: 40 calories, 0g. fat, 0g. cholesterol, 20mg sodium, 9g carbohydrates.
Kim Francis

Orange Slush

½   gallon fat-free vanilla yogurt
½   c. skim milk

1   c. frozen orange juice
     concentrate, thawed

Place half of each ingredient in a blender. Cover and blend at medium speed for about 50 seconds, until thick and smooth. Pour mixture into glasses. Repeat with remaining ingredients. Serves 8, about one cup each, 260 calories, 2g fat, 10mg cholesterol, 120mg sodium, 50g carbohydrates, 10g protein.
Melissa Martinez

Pineapple Lemon-Limeade

½   c. sugar
3   c. pineapple juice
¼   c. lemon juice

¼   c. lime juice
1   liter sparkling water, chilled
     lemon and lime slices

Mix all ingredients except sparkling water in a large pitcher and refrigerate until chilled. Just before serving, add sparkling water. Pour over ice and garnish with lemon and lime slices. Serves 8, about one cup each, 105 calories, 0g fat, 0mg cholesterol, 15mg sodium, 26g carbohydrates, 0g protein.
Reba Darby

Hot Holiday Cider

6	c. apple cider	1/4	tsp. ground nutmeg
1/2	tsp. whole cloves	11	sticks cinnamon

Heat cider, cloves, nutmeg, and 3 sticks of cinnamon in a three-quart saucepan over medium-high heat until boiling. Reduce heat to low and simmer, uncovered, 10 minutes. Strain to remove cloves and cinnamon. Place a cinnamon stick in each mug and serve hot. Six one-cup servings, 115 calories, 0g fat, 0mg cholesterol, 10 mg sodium, 20g carbohydrates.
Patricia Ward

Punch in the Pink

1	12-z. can pink lemonade, thawed	2	10-z. pkgs. frozen raspberries, thawed, in syrup
2	pts. raspberry sherbet, 1 softened and 1 frozen	1 1/2	qts. ginger ale, chilled
4	c. water	1	lime
		1	lemon

Combine lemonade, sherbet and water, and stir to blend. Add raspberries and their syrup. Pour mixture into a punch bowl. Add ginger ale. Scoop frozen pint of sherbet into balls and float in punch. Float lemon and lime slices on top.
Dianne Lewis

Strawberry Cooler

2	c. whole strawberries	2	6-oz. containers strawberry yogurt
1	c. skim milk		

Place all but four strawberries, milk and yogurt in a blender. Cover and blend on high until smooth. Pour into glasses and garnish each with a strawberry. Makes 4 servings, each 60 calories, 0g fat, 0g cholesterol, 80mg sodium, 12g carbohydrates, 3g protein.
Beverly Galvez

Demure Daiquiri

4	T. frozen limeade concentrate	1	drop mint extract
1	c. crushed ice		maraschino cherry

Blend thawed limeade, ice and mint extract in blender for a few seconds on high. Stop and scrape sides with spatula. Continue blending until fine "snow" is formed. Serve in a cocktail glass with a short straw and garnish with a cherry. Makes one.
Ruthella Samuel

Be not forgetful to entertain strangers,
for thereby some have entertained angels unawares.
Hebrews 13:2

20 tips for healthy eating...

(continued from Page 21)

8.   **Use a non-stick spray** for pan frying and baking. Sauté meat and veggies in chicken, beef, or vegetable broth instead of oil. Bake or broil instead of frying.

9.   **Eat high-fiber foods** to fill you up, such as a bran muffin instead of a donut. Switch to whole-grain breads, whole-wheat pastas, brown rice and high fiber cereals.

10.   **Think of red meat** as a side dish on your plate.

11.   **Never skip meals.** Eat three to six times a day in smaller portions to keep from getting hungry.

12.   **Use skim milk** in soups and shakes, on cereals and in recipes.

13.   **Use a smaller plate** to satisfy your need to see a full plate.

14.   **Reward yourself** with pleasures other than food—visit a friend, see a movie, take a trip, or buy a new pair of shoes.

15.   **Use sugar substitutes** – within reason – when sweetening foods and beverages.

16.   **Allow yourself a little fat.** Fat improves taste, helps you feel full, and helps maintain blood sugar levels for steady energy.

20.   **Serve up extra veggies...** pile on the bell peppers, onion, garlic, and spinach on pizzas and salads, in sandwiches and soups – so you get your healthy share!

20 tips for healthy eating...

1. **Begin a breakfast habit** to balance your diet.

2. **Go for the good stuff!** Shop the grocery's outside aisles first, where you'll find fresh fruits, veggies and whole grain breads.

3. **Take your time.** Studies show it takes about 20 minutes for your brain to realize you're not hungry anymore.

4. **Eat more fish.** Results of a study of 80,000 nurses show that those who eat fish five or more times a week had half the number of strokes as those who ate fish only one to three times a month.

5. **Think of the rainbow.** Put lots of different colors on your plate to be sure you get at least five daily servings of fruits and vegetables.

6. **Know your fats.**

    ❖ **Saturated fats** in fatty cuts of meat and full-fat dairy products, are bad for your arteries, raising the level of LDL(low-density lipoprotein) cholesterol.

    ❖ **Trans fats,** (partially hydrogenated vegetable oils) found in commercial baked goods and fried foods, raise levels of LDL (bad) cholesterol AND decrease HDL (good) cholesterol.

    ❖ **Monounsaturated fat,** found in nuts, olive and canola oils, can reduce your blood cholesterol when substituted for saturated and trans fats.

    ❖ **Polyunsaturated fats** increase HDL (good cholesterol) and have a protective effect on your body. These fats have also been found to lower your risk of type 2 diabetes. The types:

    ➧ **Omega-6** fatty acid in vegetables and seeds; and

    ➧ **Omega-3** fatty acid in fishes and soy products, whole grains and leafy greens have been related to reduced death rates from heart disease and to lowering blood cholesterol.

7. **Protein and carbohydrates each have 4 calories per gram. Fat contains 9 calories per gram.** The American Heart Association has set new guidelines that emphasize a balanced diet rather than strict counting of fats grams and calories. But it's important to know that fat has more than twice as many calories as any other nutrient.

Continued on Page 22

What's a healthy serving?

Whole Grain Breads, Cereals, Rice, and Pasta

- ❖ 1 slice of whole grain bread
- ❖ About 1 cup of high fiber cereal
- ❖ $1/2$ cup of cooked cereal, rice, or pasta

Vegetables

- ❖ 1 cup of raw leafy vegetables
- ❖ $1/2$ cup of other vegetables cooked or raw
- ❖ $3/4$ cup of vegetable juice

Fruits

- ❖ 1 medium apple, banana, orange, pear
- ❖ $1/2$ cup of chopped, cooked, or canned fruit
- ❖ $3/4$ cup of fruit juice

Milk, Yogurt, and Cheeses

- ❖ 1 cup of milk or yogurt
- ❖ $1^1/2$ ounces of natural cheese (such as Cheddar)
- ❖ 2 ounces of processed cheese (such as American)

Meat, Poultry, Fish, Dry Beans, Eggs, and Nuts

- ❖ 2-3 ounces of cooked lean meat, poultry, or fish
- ❖ $1/2$ cup of cooked dry beans or $1/2$ cup of tofu equals 1 ounce of lean meat
- ❖ $2^1/2$-ounce soy burger or 1 egg equals 1 ounce of lean meat
- ❖ 2 tablespoons of peanut butter or $1/3$ cup of nuts equals 1 ounce of meat

Low-Fat Honey Mustard Chicken

4	skinless, boneless, chicken breast halves	1	T. dijon mustard
1	can fat free chicken gravy	2	tsp. honey

Spray skillet with vegetable cooking spray; heat over medium heat for 1 minute. Cook chicken 10 minutes or until browned. Set aside. Add gravy, mustard & honey. Heat to a boil. Return chicken to pan. Cover and cook over low heat 5 minutes or until done. Serve over rice or egg noodles. Calories 422, Fat 4 grams, Saturated Fat 4 grams, Cholesterol 73 mg., Sodium 553 mg. Serves 4
Jewel Dunn

Stuffed Bell Peppers

1	lb. extra lean ground beef	1/4	c. uncooked rice
1	egg	1	tbs. sugar
1	onion, chopped		salt to taste
1	bell pepper, chopped		pepper to taste
1	large can tomato sauce, divided		water
2	cans diced tomatoes		4-6 bell peppers

Cut off tops of bell peppers and remove seeds, set aside. Combine ground meat, egg, onion, bell pepper, some tomato sauce, uncooked rice, salt and pepper. Mix well and stuff peppers with meat mixture. In a pan, combine can tomatoes, remainder of tomato sauce, sugar, 1 can water and salt and pepper. Add peppers and cook on low until done. Serves 4-6. Exchange, 1 starch, 1 lean meat., calories, 166.
Rhoda Cavin

Mexican Casserole

10	oz. cooked ground turkey	1	tsp. grated garlic	
1/2	c. green pepper, diced		Salt and pepper to taste	
1	medium onion, chopped	2	c. cooked rice	
1	pkg. chili seasoning mix	8	oz. jalapeno cheese, grated	
2	c. canned tomatoes			

Brown meat in skillet, add onions and peppers. Simmer 5 minutes, add chili seasoning, tomatoes, salt, pepper and garlic. Simmer until liquid is gone. Stir in rice, add cheese (reserve some for top) Stir together until cheese is melted. Bake in 350 degree oven 15 minutes in 9" X 13" casserole dish. This is a Weight Watchers recipe that serves 4 large helpings, counting 41/2 points each. Exchange: 1 starch, 21/2 lean meat.; calories, 224.
Margie Musick

Philip's Marinated & Roasted Chicken

4	boneless, skinless chicken breast halves	1	tsp. of garlic powder
		1	tsp. of onion powder
1	cup dry white wine	1	tsp. of coarse ground black pepper
1	jigger of lime juice		Salt to taste
1	jigger of sesame oil		
1	tsp. heaping of cayenne (less for not so spicy)		

Combine all ingredients except meat in baking dish large enough to hold meat too. Add meat to marinade liquid; slosh around to cover meat. Rest in refrigerator for at least one hour, stirring liquid and turning meat occasionally. Preheat oven to 375 degrees. Drain marinade from meat and place baking dish containing drained meat into oven; bake uncovered for 45 minutes. Serves 4. Exchange, 1 meat.
Philip Beekley

Chicken Supreme

3	c. cooked chicken, cubed
1¹/₂	c. small, diced celery
8	oz. water chestnuts, sliced
1¹/₂	c. silvered almonds, toasted
2	tsp. cajun seasoning
¹/₈	tsp. pepper
2	T. minced onion
2	T. fresh lemon juice (no substitutes)
1	can condensed cream of chicken soup

¹/₂ c. (generous) light mayonnaise

Fold in before adding topping:
8 oz. French fried onions

Topping
1¹/₂ c. herb seasoned stuffing mix, crushed, not cubed
¹/₂ c. melted butter

Combine all ingredients through lemon juice in a large mixing bowl and gently fold together. Combine the soup and mayonnaise, then fold it carefully into other ingredients. At this point, you may place in a buttered 9"X13" dish, seal well, and refrigerate overnight.

Before baking, fold in lightly the onions and cover the top with the combined stuffing mix and butter. Bake at 350 degrees for 30 minutes. When serving, top each portion with a sprinkling of minced parsley for a bit of color. Exchanges: 2 starch, 3 medium-fat meat, calories 475.
Joan Becker

Make it light! Substitute with fat-free mayonnaise and low-fat soup. Omit topping recipe. Instead, sprinkle with seasoned breadcrumbs and a drizzle of olive oil.

> The most remarkable thing about my mother is that for 30 years she served nothing but leftovers. The original meal has never been found.
> *Calvin Trillin*

Black Bean Burritos

1	T. vegetable oil	1	11 oz. can corn, drained
1	medium onion, chopped	6	8 inch flour tortillas
2	cloves of garlic, minced	3/4	c. reduced fat cheddar cheese
1 1/2	tsp. chili powder		(6 ounces), shredded
1/2	tsp. cumin	2	green onions thinly sliced
3	c. brown rice, cooked	1/4	c. plain low fat yogurt
1	16 oz. can black beans, drained and rinsed	1/4	c. prepared salsa

Heat oil in large skillet over medium-high heat until hot. Add onion, garlic, chili powder and cumin. Sauté 3 to 5 minutes until onion is tender. Add rice, beans and corn, and cook, stirring, 2 to 3 minutes until mixture is thoroughly heated. Remove from heat. Spoon 1/2 cup of rice mixture down center of each tortilla. Top each with 2 tablespoons cheese, 1 tablespoon green onion and 1 tablespoon yogurt. Roll up tortilla and top with 1 tablespoon salsa. Serves 6, exchange 1 lean meat, 2 starch, calories 275.

Jeff Boler

Laughter is the shortest distance
between two people.
Victor Borge

Venison Bake

1	lb. ground venison or beef	1/2	tsp. chili powder
1	large chopped onion	1/2	tsp. greek seasoning
16	oz. can cajun tomatoes	1/2	tsp. black pepper
16	oz. can ranch style beans, undrained		salt and garlic to taste
1	can whole kernel corn, undrained	1 1/2	c. pre-cooked rice
		1/2	c. grated cheese

Cook ground meat and onions in skillet; Add remaining ingredients except cheese and cook 15 min. (covered); Add cheese and cook until melted. Serves 6. Exchange, 1 meat, 1 starch, 2 vegetable. Calories, 260.
Stan Musick

Party Salad Sandwiches

3/4	c. chicken or tuna	16	bread slices (cut in rounds)
1/2	c. finely chopped celery	1	large can pineapple slices (dry)
1/4	c. finely chopped nuts		
1	T. lemon juice	1	large cream cheese
1/2	tsp. curry (optional)	1	cottage cheese
1/3	c. mayonnaise		

Mix first 6 ingredients. Cut bread into rounds with pineapple can and butter lightly. Mix cream and cottage cheese using pineapple juice to make a spreading consistency. Layer pineapple slice, bread filling, and bread, then ice like a cake and refrigerate. Decorate if desired. Each step may be prepared the day before and put together on the day served. For more nutritional value, use whole-grain bread. Serves 8. Exchange, 1 lean meat, 2 bread, 1/2 fruit, 1 fat.
Audrey Spanutius

Golden Catfish Fillets

1	egg white		$1/4$ to $1/2$ tsp. cayenne pepper	
1	c. milk		$1/8$	tsp. pepper
1	c. cornmeal		4	catfish fillets
$3/4$	tsp. salt			cooking oil $1/4$ inch in large
$1/4$	tsp. salt			skillet
$1/4$	tsp. garlic powder			

In a shallow bowl, beat the egg white until foamy; add milk and mix well. In another shallow bowl combine all dry ingredients. Dip fillets in milk mixture and then coat with cornmeal mixture. Heat the oil and fry over medium high for 3 – 4 minutes per each side or until it flakes easily with a fork. Serves 4. Exchange, 1 medium-fat meat, $1/4$ starch, calories 280. *Aileen Cantrell*

Quick Enchilada Casserole

1	lb. extra lean ground meat	1	can enchilada sauce (hot	
$1/2$	c. chopped onions		or mild)	
1	can cream of chicken Soup	$1/2$	can water	
1	can condensed cream of	$1/2$	lb. longhorn cheese, grated	
	mushroom Soup	1	pkg. of 10 white corn	
			tortillas (torn into pieces)	

Brown in large skillet meat and onions; Add chicken and mushroom soup, enchilada sauce and water, simmer for 15 minutes; Place 1/3 of tortillas in bottom of 9"X12" casserole dish or pan. Top with meat mixture, then grated cheese, making three layers. Bake 20 to 30 minutes at 325 degrees. Serves 4-6. Exchange, 1 bread, 1 vegetable, 2 medium-fat meat. *Marguerite J. Ross*

Hot Chicken Salad

4	c. diced cooked chicken	3	green onions (2 if large) chopped
1/2	c. diced celery	1	heaping cup mayonnaise
1½	c. diagonal silvered celery	4	T. lemon juice
1	c. sliced almonds	1½	c. potato chips, crumbled
1	small can sliced water chestnuts drained	1	8 oz. package of Colby/Monterey Jack
2	tsp. salt		cheese, grated
1	can artichoke hearts drained and chopped		

Mix all together; Bake at 375 degrees, for 30 minutes. Serve with fresh fruit salad and croissants. Serves 8. Exchange, 1 medium-fat meat, 1/2 vegetable, calories 425.
Nona Sherrill

Make it light! Try reduced-calorie mayonnaise and cheese. Sprinkle with herbed breadcrumbs instead of potato chips.

Chicken Tortilla Soup

4	cooked chicken breasts, chopped	2	c. water
		1	tsp. each cumin, chili powder, salt
15	oz. can diced tomatoes		
10	oz can enchilada sauce	1/4	tsp. pepper
1	tsp. onion powder	1	bay leaf
4	oz. diced tomatoes with green chilies	10	oz. frozen corn
		1	c. mild salsa
1	tsp. garlic powder	14½	oz can chicken broth

Put all in a crock pot and cook on low for 6–8 hours or high for 3–4 hours. When ready to serve, top each bowl with chips, avocado slices and Parmesan cheese. Serves 6-8. Exchange, 1 lean meat, 1 starch, 1 vegetable, calories, 175.
Nona Sherril and Susan Pietro

Saucy One-Pan Ravioli

2	c. cherry tomatoes	2	T. snipped fresh Basil
1	clove garlic	1	T. snipped fresh Italian
³/₄	c. chicken broth		Parsley
¹/₄	tsp. salt	¹/₄	c. shredded Romano or
¹/₄	tsp. pepper		Parmesan cheese
1	9 oz pkg. refrigerated ravioli		

In a blender or food processor bowl place tomatoes and garlic. Cover; blend or process until smooth. Transfer to a large saucepan. Add broth, salt and pepper. Bring to boiling. Add ravioli; return to boiling. Reduce heat; cover and simmer for 6 to 8 minutes or until pasta is just tender, stirring gently once or twice. Stir in basil and parsley. Spoon on to plates, sprinkle with cheese. Makes 2 servings. Calories, 283; 11 g. protein, 56 g. carbohydrates, 2g. fat.
Doris J. Seibold

Scogin's Simmered Steak Dinner

1¹/₂	lbs. round steak	1	can stewed tomatoes
1	can peas	1	T. steak sauce
1	can carrots (slices)		

Brown round steak (cut into 2¹/₂" pieces), add other ingredients and simmer at least an hour. Serve over rice, cornbread or biscuits. Makes 4–6 servings. Exchanges, 2 meat, 1 vegetable, 348 calories.
John Scogin

In the childhood memories of every good cook, there's a large kitchen, a warm stove, a simmering pot and a MOM.
Barbara Costikyan

Sautéed Chicken Breast in Cream Sauce

2	whole chicken breasts, split, skinned and boned	$^1/_8$	tsp. dried thyme, crushed
2	T. margarine	$^1/_3$ to $^3/_4$	c. dry white wine or sherry, divided
$1^1/_2$	c. thinly sliced mushrooms	1	8oz. package cream cheese, cubed
1	c. thinly sliced celery		
$^1/_2$	medium–size onion, thinly sliced	$^1/_4$	c. milk
		$2^1/_2$	c. corkscrew pasta, freshly cooked and drained
$^1/_2$	tsp. pepper		Chopped parsley, for garnish
$^1/_2$	tsp. dried basil, crushed		
$^1/_2$	tsp. dried chervil, crushed		

Cut chicken into strips. Melt margarine in a large skillet over low heat. Add chicken, mushrooms, celery, onion, pepper, basil, chervil and thyme. Cook over medium heat, stirring occasionally for 10 minutes or until the chicken is tender. Add 2 tablespoons of wine, reduce the heat and simmer for 5 minutes. Combine cream cheese and milk in a small saucepan, stir over low heat until smooth. Blend in enough of the remaining wine to make the sauce a pouring consistency. To serve, place the hot pasta on a serving platter. Top with the chicken mixture and pour the cream sauce over all. Sprinkle with chopped parsley. Makes 4–6 servings. Calories, 298, 10 g. fat.
Fely Reyes

Make it light! Sauté chicken in olive oil instead of margarine. Use fat-free cream cheese and skim milk to cut cholesterol and fat.

Time for a little something.
Winnie-the-Pooh

Linguini with White Clam Sauce

¹/₄	c. olive oil	1	tsp. sweet basil
3	finely chopped garlic cloves	4	T. fresh chopped parsley
2	cans undrained minced clams		Salt & fresh ground pepper
1	bottle clam juice		to taste
¹/₂	cup white wine (optional)	1	1b linguini
1¹/₂	tsp. oregano		

Sauté chopped garlic cloves over medium heat until they begin to turn golden brown. Slowly add the clam juice, (optional) wine, and clam liquid from cans. Bring to a boil, reduce heat and simmer to reduce liquid for 10 minutes. Add oregano, basil, salt & pepper & simmer for 5 minutes longer. Add parsley & clams stir in for 2 minutes. Pour white clam sauce over pasta & serve. Serves 5. Exchange: 2 lean meat, 1 bread, 170 calories.
Louis Johnston.

Basil Shrimp

2	T. and 1¹/₂ tsp. olive oil	3	cloves garlic, minced
¹/₄	c. butter, melted		Salt to taste
1¹/₂	lemons, juiced	1	pinch white pepper
3	T. coarse grained prepared mustard	3	pounds fresh shrimp, peeled and de-veined
¹/₄	pound minced fresh basil		

In a shallow, non-porous dish or bowl, mix together olive oil and melted butter. Then stir in lemon juice, mustard, basil and garlic, and season with salt and white pepper. Add shrimp, and toss to coat. Cover, and refrigerate for 1 hour. Preheat grill to high heat. Remove shrimp from marinade and thread on skewers. Lightly oil grate and arrange skewers on grill. Cook for 4 minutes, turning once, until done. Serves 6. Exchange, 4 meat, 1 fat; 327 calories.
Patricia Ward

Chicken and Pasta

1	tsp. olive oil	10	fresh mushrooms, quartered or sliced
2	skinless, boneless chicken breast cut in strips	2	cloves garlic, mashed
1	14.5 oz. can Italian style diced tomatoes	1	envelope Lipton Onion Recipe soup mix Spaghetti for 2

Brown chicken in olive oil in a non-stick skillet. Stir in tomatoes, mushrooms and garlic. Add onion soup mix. Simmer, covered over low heat for 15 minutes until chicken is tender. Exchange, 1 meat, 1 vegetable, 1 bread, 320 calories.
Dorothy Hoban

Penne with Portobello Mushrooms

1/4	lb. Portobello mushrooms cut into 1/4 inch slices	1	lb. penne
12	garlic cloves, sliced	2	T. unsalted butter
8	T. olive oil	3	T. finely grated Parmesan cheese
	Salt and freshly ground pepper	4	cooked artichoke bottoms; if using canned rinse well

Heat oven to 375 degrees; Put mushrooms in roasting pan with 2 cloves. Pour 2 tablespoons over and season with salt and pepper. Roast 15 minutes or till tender and garlic is soft. Meanwhile put the artichokes, 2 Tablespoons of cheese, 2 tablespoons of olive oil & a garlic clove in blender and puree adding the rest of oil, salt and pepper. Cook penne till al dente and drain. Return to pot and add butter and artichoke sauce. Toss with pasta. Season. Transfer to serving bowls and top with mushrooms and garlic. Sprinkle remaining cheese over top and serve. Serves 4-6. Exchange, 2 vegetables, 1 bread, 295 calories.
Mamie Medlin

Never eat more than you can lift.
Miss Piggy

Garden Tuna Salad

6½	oz. can water packed tuna, drained and flaked	1	T. chopped green onion Dash each of salt, pepper and
¼	c. plain non-fat yogurt or low calorie mayonnaise		garlic powder Lettuce, tomato and
2	tsp. lime or lemon juice		cucumber slices
1	tsp. poppy seed	8	slices whole grain bread

Combine tuna, yogurt or mayonnaise, lime or lemon juice, poppy seeds, onion and seasonings. Top 4 bread slices with half the lettuce. Divide tuna mixture between lettuce-topped bread slices; spread to edges. Top with tomato, cucumber slices and remaining lettuce. Top with remaining bread slices. Serves 4. 223 calories, 20 G protein, 15 g. carbohydrates, 5 g. fat, 31 mg cholesterol.
Susan Schutte

Tropical Grilled Flank Steak with Fruit Salsa

¼	c. fresh orange juice	½	tsp hot pepper sauce
2	T. chili sauce	1½	lbs. beef flank steak
2	T. soy sauce	1	medium sized orange, thinly
2	T. vegetable oil		sliced
1	tsp. sugar		Fruit Salsa (recipe follows)
1	tsp. grated orange rind		Orange wedges, for garnish
2	cloves garlic, very finely chopped		Cilantro sprigs, for garnish

Combine the orange juice, chili sauce, soy sauce, oil, sugar, orange rind, garlic, salt and hot pepper sauce in a small bowl. Place the flank steak in a plastic bag; add the orange juice mixture, turning to coat the steak. Place the orange slices on top of the steak. Close the bag securely and marinate in the refrigerator for 3 hours or overnight, turning occasionally. Pour off the marinade and orange slices and discard. Grill steak on a hot charcoal grill for 10 to 14 minutes or to desired degree of doneness, turning once. Meanwhile prepare the Fruit Salsa. Carve the steak across the grain into thin slices. Serve with the salsa and garnish with orange wedges and cilantro.

Fruit Salsa

1/2	c. diced pineapple	1/4	c. diced green bell peppers
1/2	c. diced mango	2	T. rice vinegar or white wine
1/2	c. diced green apple		vinegar
1/2	c. diced papaya	4	tsp. sugar
1/4	c. diced red bell peppers	1/4	tsp. crushed red pepper

Combine all ingredients. Cover and refrigerate before serving. If you wish, the salsa may be prepared a day in advance. Serves 6, 275 calories, 22 g. protein, 14 g. carbohydrates, 12 g. fat, 58 mg cholesterol.
Fely Reyes

Baked Chicken with Sherry-Peach Sauce

8	bone-in, skinless chicken breast halves	1/2	c. brown sugar
		2	T. arrowroot
	Garlic powder, salt, and black pepper to taste	1	c. chili sauce
2	onions, sliced	1	c. sherry
1	c. nonfat chicken broth	1 1/2	c. sliced peaches

Place the chicken, bone side down, in a single layer in a large baking dish. Season with garlic powder, salt and pepper. Broil for several minutes, until chicken is slightly browned. Set aside. Coat a medium saucepan with non-stick spray. Cook the onion s over medium heat for 5 minutes. Add the broth, brown sugar, arrowroot and chili sauce. Turn heat to high and bring the sauce to a boil, stirring constantly. Remove pan from heat and pour the sauce over the chicken. Cover chicken with foil and bake in a preheated 350 oven for 30 minutes. Remove the foil and pour the sherry and peaches over the chicken. Bake uncovered, basting occasionally, for 30 minutes, or until chicken is cooked through. Serves 8, each serving 566 calories, 13 g. fat, 30 g. protein, 83 g. carbohydrates, 14 g. fiber, 54 mg. cholesterol.
Diana Prestwood

Pork Tenderloin Diane

1	lb. pork tenderloin, cut crosswise into 8 pieces.	1	T. Worcestershire sauce
2	T. lemon pepper	1	tsp. Dijon style mustard
2	T. butter or olive oil	1	T. Finely chopped chives or parsley
2	T. lemon juice		Whole chives, for garnish

Pound each tenderloin piece into 1-inch thick medallion; sprinkle the surfaces with lemon pepper. Melt the butter in a large heavy skillet over medium heat. Add the medallions and cook for 3 to 4 minutes. Remove the pork to a serving platter and keep warm. Add the lemon juice, Worcestershire sauce and mustard to the pan juices in the skillet. Cook stirring, until heated through. Pour the sauce over the medallions; sprinkle with chopped chives. Garnish with the whole chives. Serves 4, each 201 calories, 26 g protein, 12 g. carbohydrates, 6 g. fat, 85 mg cholesterol.
Fely Reyes

Arroz Con Pollo (Chicken with Rice)

4	chicken leg quarters (cut up at joint)	1	T. (or 2 cubes) of Chicken Flavor Bouillon
2	T. cooking oil	1	8 oz. can of tomato sauce
1	tsp. salt	1	tsp. garlic powder
2	c. uncooked long grain rice	1	tsp. ground cumin powder
1	T. cooking oil		One slice of green pepper for flavor

Brown chicken in 2 tablespoons of oil in a large Dutch oven or chicken fryer pan. Add salt, cover and simmer for 15 to 20 minutes. Brown the rice in a skillet in 1 tablespoon of oil. Add the chicken bullion cubes. Add the browned rice to the chicken; add the tomato sauce, garlic powder, ground cumin and green pepper. Cover and simmer for 20 or 25 minutes, stirring only once. Serves 4 to 6, 350 calories, 39 g. protein, 32 g. carbohydrates, 7 g. fat, 86 mg. cholesterol.
Elsa Ciminelli

Veal Parmigiana

2	lb. veal cutlets	1/4	tsp. Worcestershire sauce
2	eggs, beaten		Garlic salt to taste
1	tsp. salt and pepper	1	T. butter
3/4	c. dry bread crumbs	1/4	c. Parmesan cheese
1/2	c. olive or salad oil	1/2	lb. sliced mozzarella or Swiss
2	8 oz. cans tomato sauce		cheese
1/4	tsp. basil		

Start oven at 350 degrees; Dip cutlets in a mixture of beaten eggs, salt and pepper. Coat meat with crumbs. Heat oil in large skillet and brown veal on both sides. Transfer meat to a large baking dish. Heat tomato sauce, basil, Worcestershire sauce, garlic salt and butter together for 10 minutes. Pour over veal, sprinkle with Parmesan cheese, cover tightly and bake 30 minutes. Remove cover, place a slice of mozzarella cheese over each cutlet and bake 10 minutes longer, or until cheese melts and bubbles. Serves 6-8. Exchange: 4 1/2 medium-fat meat, 425 calories. *Ruthella Samuel*

Make it light! Brown veal in two tablespoons of olive oil in a non-stick skillet. Omit butter. Substitute regular cheese with partially skim or low-fat Swiss or mozzarella.

Pasta Salad

1 1/2	c. cooked corkscrew macaroni (or your choice of pasta)	1/2	medium cucumber, quartered length wise and sliced
1/3	c. reduced calorie Italian, French or Creamy Cucumber Salad Dressing	1/2	c. chopped bell pepper
		1/4	c. chopped onion
		1	c. cherry tomatoes, halved

In colander, rinse cooked macaroni with cold water, drain well. In large bowl combine pasta, vegetables and salad dressing of your choice. Toss gently. Chill 1 – 24 hours.

Note: Create a different salad each time just by varying the salad dressing for the marinade. For variations you can also add cooked shrimp, chopped ham or chicken. Calories, 153 per serving.
Donna Foshee

Fish Creole

4	fish fillets	2	T. Parsley, snipped
1/2	c. chopped onion	1/2	tsp. garlic powder
1/2	c. chopped bell pepper	1/4	tsp. salt
1/2	c. chopped celery	1/8	tsp. ground red pepper
1/4	c. water	2	T. cold water
1	16 oz. can diced tomatoes	1	T. cornstarch
1	bay leaf		

In large skillet, combine onion, bell pepper, celery and water. Bring to a boil, reduce heat, simmer covered, about 5 minutes or until vegetables are tender; Stir in drained tomatoes, bay leaf, parsley, garlic powder, salt and red pepper. Bring to a boil; reduce heat; Simmer, covered for 5 minutes, add fish. Cook until fish just flakes when tested with a fork (allow 4 – 6 minutes per 1/2" thickness of fish). With slotted spatula, transfer fish to platter. Cover to keep warm. Stir together water and cornstarch. Stir into tomato mixture. Cook and stir until thickened. Discard bay leaf. Serve over fish. Serve over hot cooked rice, if desired. Calories 157. Serves 4.
Donna Foshee

Crunchy Chicken Bake

1	envelope cream of chicken soup mix	1/2	c. dry breadcrumbs or crushed herb seasoned stuffing mix
1/3	c. hot water		
1	whole chicken breast, split	1	T. butter or margarine, melted

Preheat oven to 375. In medium bowl, blend soup mix with water. Dip chicken in soup mixture, then in breadcrumbs. Place chicken in a baking dish and drizzle with butter. Bake 45 minutes or until tender. Recipe can be doubled. Serves 2, each 205 calories.
Elva Zerda

Chicken Lo Mien

1/4	c. green onions, thinly sliced	1	c. bean sprouts
1	tsp. minced, pared ginger root	1	tsp. light soy sauce
8	oz. chicken breast, skinned	1	tsp. oyster sauce
	and boneless cut into strips	1	c. cooked vermicelli or thin
1	c. sliced fresh mushrooms		spaghetti

Sauté green onions and ginger root in a large skillet coated with cooking spray. Add chicken strips and sauté until cooked. Add mushrooms and bean sprouts. Cook until vegetables are crisp. Stir in soy sauce and oyster sauce. Add vermicelli and stir well until all is thoroughly mixed and heated through. Serves 2, each 295 calories; exchange, 1 meat, 1 vegetable, 1 bread.
Louise Cisarik

Ground Turkey and Black Bean Chili

1	T. olive oil	2	tsp. ground cumin
2	c. finely chopped bell pepper	1	lb. ground turkey
1	c. finely chopped onion	2	(15 – 16oz each) cans black
1/2	c. finely chopped carrot		beans, rinsed and drained
2	large cloves garlic, minced	3	c. chicken broth
4	tsp. chili powder	1	T. tomato paste

Heat oil in heavy large saucepan or Dutch oven over medium-low heat. Add bell pepper, onion, carrot and garlic; sauté until tender, about 12 minutes. Add chili powder and cumin; stir to blend. Increase heat to medium-high and add turkey; break up with a spoon and sauté until turkey is no longer pink, about 3 minutes. Add beans, broth and tomato paste; bring to a boil. Reduce heat and simmer chili until liquid thickens, stirring occasionally, about 1 hour. Season with salt and pepper. Serves 4-6; 325 calories, 42 g. carbohydrates, 29 g. protein, 55 mg. cholesterol, 5 g. fat.
Susan Schutte

> Wish I had time for one last bowl of chili.
> *Kit Carson's last words*

Baked Pork Chops

1	can cream of mushroom soup	1/2	pkg. dry onion soup
1/2	soup can water	6	pork loin chops

Brown pork chops in oiled skillet. Put in casserole pan. Mix soup, water, and onion soup together; pour over pork chops & cover tightly. Bake at 350 degrees for 2 hours. Serves 6, each 250 calories, 11 g. carbohydrates, 29 g. protein, 9 g. fat.
Dolores Ohnemus

Make it light! Trim all fat off chops and use low-fat mushroom soup in this recipe.

Macaroni and Cheese

8	oz. elbow macaroni or twists	1	c. (4 oz.) shredded sharp cheddar cheese
16	oz. container low fat (1%) cottage cheese	1	tsp. salt
2	T. all purpose flour	1/4	tsp. black pepper
2	c. skim milk	1/4	tsp. nutmeg
		1/4	c. Parmesan cheese

Prepare macaroni as label directs but do not add salt to the water; drain. Preheat oven to 375 degrees; spray a shallow, broiler safe 2½ quart casserole with a non-stick spray. In food processor with knife blade attached, blended cottage cheese until smooth. In a 2-quart saucepan, mix flour with 1/4 cup milk until smooth. Slowly stir in remaining 1³/₄ cup milk until blended. Cook over medium heat until mixture just boils and thickens slightly, stirring frequently. Remove saucepan from heat; stir in cottage cheese, cheddar cheese, salt, pepper and nutmeg. Place macaroni in prepared casserole dish. Pour cheese sauce over macaroni. Bake, uncovered, for 20 minutes. Remove casserole from the oven. Turn oven to broil. Sprinkle Parmesan cheese on top of macaroni mixture. Place casserole in oven under broiler at closest position to source of heat; broil 2-3 minutes or until top is golden brown. Serves 4, each 375 calories, 51 g carbohydrates, 31 g. protein, 7 g. fat.
Susan Schute

Taco Soup

1	lb. ground beef	1¹/₂	c. water
3	cans chili beans, with juice	1	can chopped green chilies
1	can whole kernel corn, with juice	1	pkg. taco seasoning mix
1	can chopped tomatoes, with juice	1	pkg. ranch dressing mix

Brown beef in large pot. Stir remaining ingredients into beef mixture and cook over medium heat until heated through. This recipe works well in a crock pot, and is easy to fix on a camping trip. The leftovers can be frozen up to 3 months. Exchange: 1 medium-fat meat, 1/2 starch, 1 vegetable.
Sally Burns

Make it light! After browning the beef, drain in a colander and return to pan, then add remaining ingredients.

Chicken Pot Pie

2	large chicken breast halves	1/2	c. frozen peas
1	14-1/2 oz. can chicken broth	2-3	T. cornstarch
2	carrots		Salt and pepper to taste
1/2	onion		2 ready-made pie crusts
1	potato		

Boil chicken until tender, about 30 minutes; dice and set aside. Chop carrots, onion and potato. Cook vegetables in chicken broth until tender for about 15 minutes; add peas. Dilute cornstarch with water and add to vegetables and broth; mix until bubbly. Add chicken, salt and pepper Fill bottom pie crust with mixture, then top with other crust. With a sharp knife, make slits in top crust. Bake according to pie crust directions and enjoy. Serves 6, each 350 calories; exchange: 1 meat, 1 vegetable, 2 bread.
Evelyn Smith

Spinach Pesto Pasta

1²/₃	c. firmly packed, fresh spinach leaves	¹/₂	c. coarsely chopped pecans
³/₄	c. picante sauce	¹/₃	c. olive oil
²/₃	c. grated Parmesan cheese	1	clove minced garlic
		1	lb. cooked pasta

Combine spinach, ¹/₄ cup picante sauce, cheese, pecans, oil and garlic in bowl of food processor or blender container; process with steel blade or blend until smooth. Transfer to small bowl; stir in remaining picante sauce. Toss spinach mixture with hot cooked pasta; sprinkle with additional chopped pecans, if desired, and serve with additional pace picante sauce. Serves 6, each 225 calories; exchange: 2 starch, 1 vegetable, 1 fat.
Kathleen Childs

One-Pot Spaghetti

1	lb. ground beef or turkey	¹/₂	tsp. sugar
1	medium onion, chopped	¹/₂	tsp. salt
2	c. water	1	pkg. (8 oz.) long spaghetti
1	can (8oz.) tomato sauce	3	T. Parmesan cheese
1	jar (14-15oz) spaghetti sauce with mushrooms		

In Dutch oven, over medium heat, cook ground beef until brown, stirring often. Drain. Stir into beef the onion, water, tomato sauce, spaghetti sauce, sugar and salt. Add spaghetti to beef mixture. Heat mixture to boiling over medium-high heat, stirring a few times to keep spaghetti from sticking. Turn heat to low. Cover and simmer about 15 minutes or until spaghetti is tender. Remove from heat and stir. Sprinkle with Parmesan cheese. Serves 4; 325 calories; 9 g. fat.
Helen Murphy

No one is lonely eating spaghetti;
it requires so much attention.
Christopher Morley

Chicken Parmesan Risotto

1	T. canola oil	1²/₃	c. of 2% milk
1	lb. boneless, skinless chicken breasts cut into small pieces	¹/₂	c. grated Parmesan cheese
		¹/₂	tsp. Italian seasoning (optional)
1	large tomato		
1	can (10-3/4 oz.) cream of chicken soup (low fat)	2	c. minute white rice uncooked

Heat oil in skillet, add chicken, and cook until lightly brown. Chop tomato and set aside; add soup, milk, parmesan cheese and seasoning. Stir, then heat to a boil. Stir in rice and tomato; cover and cook on low heat 5 minutes, or until cooked through. Serves 4; 315 calories; 3 g. fat.
Evelyn Smith

Restaurant-Style Chicken Tenderloins

1	lb. skinless, boneless chicken breast	1	tsp. fresh lime juice
¹/₂	c. Italian-style salad dressing	1¹/₂	tsp. honey
		2	T. canola oil

Slice chicken into thin strips. In a small bowl mix together the dressing, lime juice and honey. Place chicken strips in a 9x13-inch baking dish and pour mixture over chicken, covering all. Cover dish and refrigerate for 1 hour. Remove chicken from marinade, discarding any remaining marinade. Heat oil in a large skillet over medium heat and sauté chicken strips until lightly browned and cooked through, 12 to 15 minutes. Serves 4, each 235 calories, 2 g. fat.
Veronica Laurel

Crispy Crunchy Chicken

2¹/₂ to 3	lb. chicken pieces, skinned	¹/₄	tsp. thyme
1	c. buttermilk	¹/₄	tsp. salt
¹/₂	tsp. garlic powder	2	c. cornflakes, finely crushed
¹/₂	tsp. paprika		

Dip chicken pieces into buttermilk; combine all spices and crushed corn-flakes in a bag; shake chicken pieces in the bag until coated; place in 9x13 inch baking dish; Bake at 350 degrees for 1 to 1¹/₂ hours or until juices run clear. Serves 6, each 204 calories;, 35 g. protein, 8 g. carbohydrates, 2 g. fat.
Donna Foshee

Red Beans and Rice

1	c. red beans, dried	4	oz. andouille or smoked
2	tsp. olive oil		sausage, diced (optional)
1/2	large onion, chopped	1/2	tsp. dried thyme
3	cloves garlic, minced	1/4	tsp. cayenne pepper
6	oz. boneless smoked pork	3 1/2	c. water
	chops, diced	1	c. steamed rice

Soak the beans overnight in enough water to cover them; heat the olive oil in a large, heavy bottomed pot over medium heat. Add the onion and garlic and sauté until tender, about 6 minutes. Stir in the pork chop pieces, sausage, thyme and cayenne and sauté for 2 minutes. Add the beans and 3 1/2 cups of water. Simmer over low heat until the beans are creamy, about 1 1/2 hours. Serve with steamed rice. Serves 4, each 201 calories; exchange 1 meat, 2 starch; 4 fat grams.
Alice Buske

Low-Fat Fettuccine Alfredo

1	c. 2% milk	3	cloves garlic, minced
2	T. all purpose flour	1/4	c. Parmesan cheese
2	T. light margarine	1	lb. fettuccine, cooked and
1/2	tsp. salt		drained

Mix all ingredients except fettuccine in 1/2 qt. Microwave safe bowl. Cook uncovered 2 minutes on high; stir and cook 1-2 minutes longer on high, stirring after 1 minute until thick; stir in cooked fettuccine and microwave 1-2 minutes until hot. Serves 6, each 325 calories, 9 g. fat.
Donna Foshee

Meat & Potato Pie

1	can condensed cream of mushroom soup	2	T. chopped parsley
1	lb. lean ground beef	1/4	tsp. salt
1/4	c. finely chopped onion		Dash of pepper
1	egg, slightly beaten	2	c. prepared mashed potatoes
1/4	c. fine dry bread crumbs	1/4	c. shredded mild cheese

Mix thoroughly 1/2 cup soup, beef, onion, egg, breadcrumbs, parsley and seasonings. Press firmly into 9 inch pie plate; Bake at 350 degrees for 25 minutes; spoon off fat; frost with potatoes; top with remaining soup and cheese; bake 10 minutes more until done; garnish with cooked sliced bacon if desired. Serves 4 to 6.
Ruth M. Botello

Make it light! Choose low-fat soup and cheese; substitute lean ground turkey for ground beef; garnish with parsley instead of bacon.

Honey Mustard Chicken

1	T. olive oil	1/2	tsp. dried tarragon or lemon pepper
1/2	c. Dijon mustard		
3	T. honey	8	skinless, boneless chicken breasts
1/2	tsp. curry		

Blend oil mustard, honey, pepper & curry; arrange chicken in 11x7x2 inch baking dish coated with no stick cooking spray; pour sauce over chicken; bake at 350 degrees for 35 minutes or until chicken is done; Serves 8, each 150 calories, 26 g. protein, 4 g. fat.
Peggy Young

> Small cheer and great welcome
> makes a merry feast.
> *William Shakespeare*

Easy Baked Stew

2	lb. lean stew meat	3	carrots, quartered
	Salt, pepper & paprika to taste	10¹/₂	oz. can condensed cream of celery soup
2	T. dry onion soup mix	¹/₂	c. water
6	med. potatoes	¹/₂	c. wine
8	white boiling onions		

Season meat with salt, pepper, paprika and onion soup mix. Place meat in Dutch oven, add whole potatoes and onions, and then add quartered carrots. Blend celery soup with water and wine; pour over meat. Cover. Bake in slow oven (250 degrees to 300 degrees) for 5 hours. This is an especially easy recipe with no browning of meat or watching necessary. Serves 8; each 355 calories, 38 g. protein, 25 g. carbohydrates, 14 g. fat.
John Young

Tallarini

1	lb. lean ground beef	2	c. whole kernel corn
1	onion, chopped	1	c. chopped ripe olives
1¹/₂	c. tomato soup	1	c. grated cheddar cheese
1¹/₂	c. cold water		Salt and pepper to taste
2	c. uncooked wide noodles		

Brown onion and meat. Add soup, water, salt and dry noodles; mix thoroughly and cook over low heat for 15 minutes; add corn and olives; pour into a 9x13 inch baking dish coated with cooking spray; sprinkle with cheese, cover and bake for 45 – 50 minutes at 350. Serve with green salad and hot garlic bread. Makes 6 to 8 servings, each 375 calories; 12 g. fat.
E. Jeanne La Feber

Make it light! Drain the beef, or use ground turkey breast. Substitute low-fat cheese.

Stuffed Cabbage

1	green cabbage (3 lb.)	1/2	c. parmesan cheese
1	c. spinach, cooked	2	eggs, beaten
1	· T. parsley, chopped		Salt
5	T. salad oil		Pepper
1/2	lb. ground beef or turkey, cooked		

Rinse cabbage; boil whole in salted water for 5 minutes; drain well; mix together remaining ingredients except oil. Spread leaves gently; insert some stuffing and wrap until all is used. Place in baking dish and cover with oil; bake for 25 minutes at 350 degrees or until cabbages is tender. Add hot water to pan if dry. Makes 4 servings., each 1 medium-fat meat, 1 vegetable.
Patricia Ward

Microwave Turkey-Stuffed Peppers

6	medium green bell peppers	1/4	tsp. pepper
1	lb. ground turkey	1	c. low sodium tomato sauce (8 oz.)
1	c. cooked rice		
2	T. onion, minced	1/2	c. water
1	T. Worcestershire sauce	1	oz. skim mozzarella cheese, shredded
1	clove garlic, minced		

Cut off tops of green peppers; remove seeds and membrane; mix turkey with rice, onion, Worcestershire sauce, garlic, and pepper. Mix half of tomato sauce with turkey mixture, then spoon mixture into peppers; cover. Place in microwave and cook 18 to 22 minutes, giving dish quarter turn every 5 minutes. Add water and remaining tomato sauce. Sprinkle cheese over each pepper. Recover and return to microwave. Cook 1 to 2 minutes until cheese melts. Makes 6 servings, each one meat, 1 vegetable, 1 starch.
Alice Buske

Carbohydrates – Good & Bad

The one time "refined" isn't a good thing…is when it comes to carbohydrates. Most of the complex carbohydrates we eat are made from refined grains, which are stripped of their nutritious bran and germ. To our bodies, refined complex carbohydrates are virtually the same as sugar molecules that are rapidly absorbed, providing calories for energy, but not much else.

According to a report by Harvard University's School of Public Health, the difference between whole grains and refined grains can make a major difference in your risk of heart disease, diabetes, colon cancer and breast cancer.

Whole grains carry their nutrients in the bran and germ part of the grain kernels. These extra nutrients contain fiber, antioxidants, lignans (precursors to weak forms of estrogen that are linked to lower rates of breast cancer), and trace minerals such as zinc and selenium that help strengthen the immune system.

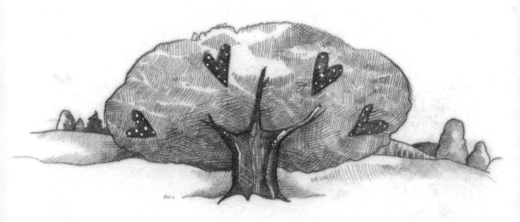

LIFE'S GARDEN PLOTS

Plant three rows of peas:
Peace of mind,
Peace of heart,
Peace of soul.

Plant four rows of squash:
Squash gossip,
Squash indifference,
Squash grumbling,
Squash selfishness.

Plant four rows of lettuce:
Lettuce be faithful,
Lettuce be kind,
Lettuce be patient,
Lettuce really love one another.

No garden can be without turnips:
Turnip for meetings,
Turnip for service,
Turnip to help one another.

Water freely with patience and cultivate with love.
There is much fruit in your garden
Because you reap what you sow.

To conclude our garden we must have thyme:
Thyme for God,
Thyme for each other,
Thyme for family,
Thyme for friends.

Submitted by Beth Prater

Grilled Corn and Black Bean Salad

3	ears shucked corn	2	tsp sugar
1/2	c. fresh lime juice (about 2 limes)	2	tsp. ground cumin
		2	tsp. chili powder
1/3	c. minced red onion	1	15-oz. can black beans,
1/3	c. minced fresh cilantro		drained
3	T. white vinegar		Lime wedges (optional)

Preheat grill. Place corn on a grill rack, grill 20 minutes or until corn is lightly browned, turning every 5 minutes. Cool. Cut kernels from corn, place in a bowl. Add juice and remaining ingredients, stir gently. Cover and chill for 1 hour. Garnish with lime wedges, if desired. Yield 6 servings (serving size: 1/2 cup), each 98 calories, 0.8 g. fat, 5 g. protein, 23 g. carbohydrates, 5 g. carbohydrates.
Patricia Ward

Corn Pudding

1	15 1/4-oz. can whole kernel corn, drained	2	beaten eggs
		1/4	c. margarine or butter, melted
1	14 3/4-oz. can cream-style corn	1/4	tsp. pepper
1	c. milk	1/2	c. cornmeal

In a large mixing bowl combine whole kernel corn, cream-style corn, milk, eggs, melted margarine or butter, and pepper. Add cornmeal, stir until moistened.

Pour corn mixture into a 2-quart casserole dish. Bake casserole in a 350 degree oven for 50 to 55 minutes or until lightly browned and set in the center. Makes 8 side-dish servings, each 250 calories.
Fr. Bob Lampert

Sauerkraut Salad

1	c. sugar	1	green bell pepper, seeded and chopped
1/2	c. white wine vinegar		
1/2	c. vegetable oil	1	jar (4 to 5 oz.) pimento, chopped
1	jar (32 oz.) sauerkraut, rinsed and well drained		Salt and freshly ground pepper to taste
2 to 3 ribs celery, chopped			
1	lg. onion, chopped		

In a small pan, simmer the sugar and vinegar until the sugar is dissolved. Stir in the oil. Squeeze the drained sauerkraut inn a clean towel to remove the remaining moisture. Combine the sauerkraut, celery, onion, bell pepper and pimento in a large glass or enameled metal bowl. Add the sauce and thoroughly toss to combine. Salt and pepper to taste. Refrigerate overnight before serving. Grated apples or carrots may be added as well as a teaspoon or two of caraway seeds if desired. Serves 6-8, each 175 calories.
Phyllis Kannowski

Make it light! Reduce amount of sugar and oil by half.

German Slaw

1	lg. head cabbage, shredded	1	c. oil
1	lg. onion, sliced or chopped	2	T. salt
1	c. sugar	1	T. celery seed
1	c. vinegar	1	T. mustard seed

Mix cabbage, onion and sugar and let set. Bring remaining ingredients to a boil. Pour over cabbage mixture and stir well. Let set in refrigerator for 4-6 hours before serving. Will keep up to 2 months in a tight container. Serves 8, each 175 calories.
Kathleen Childs

Chicken Dijon Pasta Salad

4	oz. rotini pasta, uncooked	1	c. chicken breast, cooked
8	oz. plain low-fat yogurt		and diced
1/3	c. wheat germ	3/4	c. broccoli flowerets, diced
3	T white wine vinegar	1/2	c. tomato, chopped and
1	T. Dijon mustard		seeded
1/8	tsp. black pepper	1/3	c. red onion, chopped

Cook pasta according to package directions.
In medium bowl, combine yogurt, wheat germ, vinegar, mustard and pepper; mix well. Add pasta and remaining ingredients, toss to coat. Serve immediately or chill before serving. Sprinkle with additional wheat germ before serving. Serves 4 Food Exchange per serving: 1 Lean-meat exchange + 1 vegetable exchange + 1 starch exchange. Per serving: Cal 260; Cholesterol 35mg; Carbohydrates 34g; Protein 22g.
Christie Galvin

Tuna & Wild Rice Salad

3	med. cans water-pack tuna	1	pint sour cream
3	cups long grain and wild rice,	1/4	c. mayonnaise
	cooked		Sliced almonds to taste

Mix all ingredients together, chill well. Serve with crackers, or make finger sandwiches. Makes 24 finger sandwiches; each 145 calories.
Ofelia M. Alaniz

Make it light! Choose fat-free sour cream and mayonnaise.

Feta, Chicken and Asparagus Salad

1½	lbs. boneless and skinless chicken breasts	2	heads Boston lettuce	
1	tsp. salt	2	c. sliced Roma tomatoes	
1	tsp. pepper	½	c. chopped red onion	
¼	c. olive oil	½	c. crumbled Feta cheese	
3	T. lemon juice	2	tsp. fresh rosemary, finely chopped	
½	lb. asparagus cut into one-inch pieces			

Season chicken breasts with salt and pepper. Marinate chicken in oil and lemon juice for 1 hour. Grill over hot coals until done, but not dry. Slice breasts diagonally and set aside. Place asparagus in boiling water for 2 minutes, then rinse under cold water. Set aside. Divide lettuce among salad plates and top with next four ingredients. Top with grilled chicken slices and asparagus. Drizzle with Honey Mustard Vinaigrette (see below) before serving. Makes 4 to 6 servings, each 1 low-fat meat, 1 vegetable, 1 fat.

Honey Mustard Vinaigrette:
⅓ c. red wine vinegar
1 T. honey
1 T. Dijon mustard
½ c. olive oil
1 tsp. lemon pepper
1 tsp. salt

Combine all ingredients in a small bowl. Chill. Whisk before drizzling over chicken. Makes 1 cup.
Doris J. Seibold

Tell me what you eat and I will tell you what you are.
Anthelme Brillat-Savarin

Cottage Cheese Spinach Salad

1	pkg. spinach (10 oz.) fresh, torn	1/2	c. sugar
1	12-oz. container cottage cheese (small curd)	3	T. vinegar
		2	tsp. horseradish
1/2	c. chopped pecans, toasted	1/2 tsp. salt	
		1/2 tsp. ground mustard	

In a large serving bowl, layer 1/2 spinach, cottage cheese, and pecans.
Repeat layers. In a small bowl, combine the remaining ingredients.
Drizzle over salad and toss to coat. Serve immediately. Serves 10, each 55
calories; 2 g. fat.
Angela Pollack

Rosie's Mock Caesar Salad

2	cloves garlic, peeled and minced	6	c. torn Romaine lettuce (2 heads)
1/4	c. reduced-sodium soy sauce	1/8	tsp. fresh black pepper, finely cracked
1/4	c. freshly squeezed lemon juice	1	T. Parmesan cheese, freshly grated
3	c. chopped Belgian endive (4 heads)	1 1/3	c. chopped tomato (1 lg. tomato)

Put the first three ingredients in a salad bowl and whisk thoroughly.
Add the lettuce and endive. Toss to coat. Sprinkle pepper and Parmesan
on top. Garnish with chopped tomato. Serves 4, each 80 calories and
12 g. fat.
Elizabeth Edwards Killingsworth

Lime Gelatin Salad

1   6-oz. lime gelatin   1   20-oz. crushed pineapple

Mix together, bring to a boil, remove from heat. Let cool thoroughly and add:

2   c. buttermilk   1   lg. container prepared
                                                whipped topping

Put in a 9 x 13 pan and refrigerate. (For smaller amounts, cut recipe in half). Serves 10, each 45 calories, 3 g. fat.
Gale Yost

Mango Salad

2   3-oz. pkgs. lemon gelatin (2   1   26-oz. jar mangoes and juice
     c. boiling water, 1 c. cold   1   8-oz. cream cheese, softened
     water)

Dissolve gelatin in 2 cups boiling water. Stir well and then add 1 cup cold water. Puree mangoes and juice in blender, adding 8-oz. softened cream cheese and blend until smooth. Pour into mold to set.. Serves 8, each 60 calories, 5 g. fat.
Elizabeth Edwards Killingsworth

Make it light! Use fat-free cream cheese for 0 fat grams.

Orange Salad

8   oz. prepared light whipped   2   11-oz. cans mandarin
     topping   oranges (drained)
24   oz. low-fat cottage cheese   1   pkg. orange gelatin (dry)

Blend cottage cheese and orange gelatin with mixer. Add oranges and whipped topping. Refrigerate. Serves 8, each 25 calories, 3 g. fat.
Sally Burns

Creamy Carrot-Nut Mold

2	c. hot water	1	13 1/2-oz. can crushed
1	6-oz. pkg. orange gelatin		pineapple
1	c. light sour cream	1/2	c. chopped walnuts
2	c. grated carrots		

Pour hot water over gelatin, stirring until completely dissolved, add to sour cream gradually. Stir until blended. Chill until mixture begins to set, stirring several times; add carrots, pineapple and walnuts. Pour into mold and chill for about 4 hours. Serves 8, each 60 calories, 5 g. fat.
Jeanne Thompson

Marinated Vegetable Salad

3/4	c. vinegar	1	green pepper, chopped
1/2	c. vegetable oil	1	17-oz. can English peas,
1	tsp. salt		drained
1	c. sugar	1	16-oz. can French style green
1	T. water		beans, drained
1	tsp. pepper	1	12-oz. can shoe peg whole
1	c. celery, chopped		kernel corn, drained
1	bunch green onions,	1	2-oz. jar chopped pimento,
	chopped		drained

Combine first six ingredients in medium saucepan and bring to a boil, stirring to dissolve sugar. Cool. Combine vegetables and stir in cooled vinegar mixture. Cover and place in refrigerator 12 hours, stirring occasionally. Serves 8, each 120 calories, 22 g. carbohydrates, 5 g. fat.
Joan Becker

Light tomorrow with today!
Elizabeth Barrett Browning

Macaroni Shrimp Salad

1   lb. shrimp, boiled
2   c. cooked macaroni (1 c. dry
     cooked until tender)
1/2 green pepper chopped
1/2 small onion, chopped (or
     use some green onions)
3 or 4 stalks celery, chopped
2 or 3 hard-boiled eggs, chopped

Dressing
1/2 c. mayonnaise (not salad
     dressing)
     Juice of 1/2 lemon
3   T. catsup
2 or 3 tsp. horseradish

To a kettle of salted boiling water, add shrimp and cook until white, just a few minutes. Drain well; rinse with cold water. Peel shrimp. Refrigerate. Cook macaroni according to package directions, drain. Rinse with cold water and drain again. Set aside. Combine shrimp, macaroni, vegetables, and eggs. Add nearly all the dressing. Mix thoroughly. Refrigerate. Best if made a day ahead to allow flavors to blend. Serves 4 to 6, each 350 calories.
Wanda Joyner

Make it light! Use low-fat mayonnaise to cut calories and fat grams, or cut amount of mayonnaise in half for a lighter dressing.

Vegetable Confetti

1   sml. zucchini, shredded
1   sml. yellow squash, shredded
2   carrots, shredded
1   sml. onion, sliced thin
2   T. water
2   tsp. butter or margarine

Combine the zucchini, yellow squash, carrots, onion and water in a skillet. Cover and cook over medium heat for 4 to 5 minutes, or until tender. Add the butter. Sauté, uncovered, until all moisture has evaporated. Serve immediately. Serves 2. 2 vegetable exchanges, 1 fat exchange. Each serving contains: 94 calories, 14 g. carbohydrates, 3 g. protein, 4 g. fat.
Patricia Ward

ABC's of Vegetables

1	c. asparagus pieces		Vegetable cooking spray
1	c. broccoli flowerets	2	T. onions, finely chopped
1	c. carrots	1	tsp. thyme
1	c. spinach	1/2	c. water
1	11-oz. can cream of mushroom soup (condensed)		Salt to taste Fresh ground pepper

Layer asparagus, broccoli, carrots, and spinach in a baking dish covered with vegetable cooking spray. Blend remaining ingredients. Pour over vegetables. Cover. Bake at 350 degrees for 30 to 40 minutes, or until vegetables are tender. Serves 8. Food exchange per serving: 1 vegetable exchange + 1/2 starch/bread exchange + 1/2 fat exchange; Cal: 42
Heather Boler

Fairway Farm Squash

3	lbs. yellow squash	1	sml. clove garlic, crushed
1	green bell pepper, diced	1	jalapeno pepper, seeded and chopped (use 2 if you like it spicy!)
1	lg. white onion, diced		
4	stalks of celery, diced		
6	slices of bacon, cooked and crumbled	1	stick of butter
		1	c. cheddar cheese, grated
1	sml. can pimientos, diced		Bread crumbs

Cook squash, drain, and mash. Saute all remaining ingredients (except cheese) in stick of butter until soft. Add to squash and add grated cheese. Pour into baking dish, lightly cover with bread crumbs and cook at 350 degrees until bubbly. Can be made day before.
Nina Dahlstrom Stowers

> Oh, Adam was a gardener, and God who made him sees
> that half a proper gardener's work is done upon his knees.
> *Rudyard Kipling*

Scalloped Potatoes

1	lb. potatoes (about 3 med. size), pared and sliced	1/2	tsp. freshly ground pepper
2	T. all-purpose flour	2	T. butter or margarine
1/2	tsp. salt	3	T onion, finely chopped

Preheat oven to 400 degrees. Prepare a 1 1/2 qt. casserole dish with vegetable coating. Slice potatoes crosswise in 1/8-inch slices. If potatoes are large, cut slices in half. Mix together flour, salt, and pepper. Place half of the potatoes in prepared casserole. Dot with half the butter, sprinkle half the seasoned flour on top, then half the onion. Repeat layers once more. Pour enough hot water in, at one corner only, so that the water barley comes to the top of the potatoes. Cover and bake 50 minutes, then uncover and bake for 25-30 minutes or until potatoes are browned and tender. Per 1/2 cup per serving: 1 Starch Exchange + 1 Fat exchange. Cho: 17g; Pro: 2g; Fat: 5g; Cal 117; Low-sodium diets: Omit salt and use unsalted margarine. For more fiber and nutrients, leave the skin on the potatoes!
Helene Murphy

Beef Vegetable Soup

1 1/2	lbs. chuck steak	1/2	head cabbage (small head)
8	green onions and tops	1	c. uncooked macaroni – your choice
5	stalks celery		Salt, pepper, and parsley flakes to taste
6	med. carrots, peeled		
5	med. potatoes, peeled		
1	28-oz. can whole tomatoes		

Remove excess fat from steak and discard. Cut meat into bite-size pieces. Place meat and bones into a large (4 quart) pot and brown slightly. Add seasonings. While meat is browning, chop onions and celery into 1" pieces and cook gently with meat until celery is tender. Add 2 quarts water. Then cover and simmer until meat is tender. Meanwhile, cut potatoes and carrots into bite-size pieces. Dice the canned tomatoes. Add potatoes, carrots, and tomatoes to soup. Continue cooking gently while you cut the cabbage into 1/2" slices. Add cabbage and macaroni to soup. Cook slowly until carrots are tender. Remove bones. If soup is too think, add more water and adjust seasonings to taste.. Serves 8, each exchange: 1 starch, 1 vegetable, 1 medium-fat meat..
Frank J. Roznovsky

Gingered Carrots

³/₄ lb. fresh carrots
¹/₂ c. chicken broth
     Dash onion powder
2   T. fresh lemon juice

¹/₂ tsp. ground ginger
1   T. fresh parsley, chopped
1   T. whipped butter

Cut carrots in matchstick slices or thin rounds. Place in a saucepan with broth and onion powder. Cook 15 minutes or until tender. Drain, add remaining ingredients and toss lightly. Serves 2, exchange: 2 vegetables; 56 calories, 3 g. fat, 13 g. carbohydrates.
Linda McClung

Spaghetti Salad

1   lb. spaghetti, cooked and drained
1   green bell pepper, coarsely chopped
1   purple onion, coarsely chopped

1   4-oz. can sliced mushrooms
2   T. salad seasoning
1   12-oz. bottle light Italian dressing
     Parmesan cheese to taste
1   pt. of whole cherry tomatoes

Mix in a large bowl and enjoy. Serves 6, exchange: 2 vegetables, 1 starch, 4 g. fat.
Adelle Hesse

Baked Sweet Onion

1   giant Walla Walla sweet onion
1   T. olive oil

Sprinkle of fresh rosemary
Garlic salt, salt and pepper to taste

Place onion on a piece of foil large enough to wrap it. Make several cuts in a pie shape partway through the onion. Drizzle oil over the onion and sprinkle seasonings on top. Wrap in foil and bake in the oven at 350 for an hour. Wonderful with steak or barbecue. Serves 4, each 1 g. fat.
Molly Beekley

Creamy Potatoes and Cauliflower

8	lg. potatoes, peeled and quartered	1	lg. package light cream cheese, cubed
6	cloves of garlic	1	c. light sour cream
3	c. cauliflower florets (½ head)		Salt & pepper to taste
		½	c. fresh breadcrumbs
3	T. Butter	½	c. parsley, chopped fine

In a large pan with a tight-fitting lid, cook the potatoes and the garlic in ¼ cup water for 10 minutes. Add the cauliflower and simmer, covered, another 10 minutes or until very tender. Drain well. Put back on the heat to dry. Add butter, cream cheese, sour cream, and salt and pepper to taste. Mash until creamy. Spoon into a 9" x 13" greased baking dish. Combine the breadcrumbs and parsley. Sprinkle on top of the potato mixture. Dot with butter. Heat at 325 degrees, covered, for 20 minutes. Remove cover and cook for another 10 minutes, or until heated through. Serves 10, each 1 fat, 1 vegetable, 1½ starch, 235 calories.
Jeanne Thompson

Summer Squash and Zucchini Casserole

2	med. yellow summer squash, diced	1½	c. milk
1	med. zucchini, diced	2	eggs, beaten
1	sm. onion, chopped	1	c. quick-cooking rice
1½	c. shredded Monterrey Jack cheese	½	tsp. salt
		½	tsp. Italian seasoning
1	c. grated Parmesan cheese	⅛	tsp. pepper

Combine all ingredients in large bowl and mix well. Pour into greased 9" square baking dish. Bake at 375 degrees for 35 minutes or until liquid is absorbed. Serves 4, each 375 calories, 1 vegetable, 2 high-fat meat, 1 starch.
Lynn Hilger

Make it light! Choose skim milk, 3 egg whites instead of 2 eggs, and low-fat cheese.

French Onion Soup

5	cups yellow onions, thinly sliced	4 to 6	cans beef broth
3	T. butter	1/2	c. dry white wine
1	T. oil		Salt and pepper to taste
1	tsp. salt	3	T. cognac
1/4	tsp. sugar	6	slices bead
3	T. flour		Swiss cheese for garnish

In a heavy 4-qt. covered pan, cook the onions slowly in butter and oil for 15 minutes. Stir in salt and sugar and cook for 30 to 40 minutes, covered, until onions are golden brown. Sprinkle in flour and stir for 3 minutes. Remove from heat and slowly add beef bullion to onions. Add wine. Add salt and pepper to taste. Simmer partially covered for 30 to 40 minutes more. Stir in cognac and set aside, uncovered. Garnish each bowl with toasted bread rounds, drizzled with olive oil and a sprinkling of shredded Swiss cheese. Set under broiler for 1 minute. Serves 6, each 225 calories, 6 g. fat.
Jeanne Thompson

Microwave Scalloped Potatoes

	Cooking spray	1/4	c. Parmesan cheese, grated
3	med. potatoes, sliced thin (leave skins on to get more fiber, vitamins and minerals!)	3/4	c. skim milk
		1/2	tsp. paprika

Coat a 1 or 2 quart casserole dish with cooking spray. Layer potato slices and cheese. Pour milk on top and sprinkle with paprika. Cover and vent, microwave on high 10-12 minutes, rotating dish every 3 to 4 minutes. To brown, broil in oven 2 to 3 minutes. Serve immediately. Serves 2, each 145 calories.
Alice Westfall

Fresh Out-of-the-Garden Soup

6	lg. vine-ripe tomatoes, peeled and cut into small chunks	1	yellow squash, chopped
		1	ear of corn, shucked
12	okra pods, tops cut off, diced	1	garlic clove, crushed
		1/4	c. water
4	green onions, peeled and chopped	1	tsp. chili powder
		1/2	tsp. lemon juice
			Salt and pepper
2	carrots, peeled and sliced	1/2	c. shredded cheddar cheese

Cut tomatoes over a large saucepan in order to catch juice. Add all of the other ingredients except cheese. Bring mixture to almost boiling. Cook at simmer with lid on pan for 30 minutes. Last 5 minutes of cooking, stir in shredded cheese. Serves 8, each 260 calories.
JoAnn

Baked Spinach Squares

3	eggs, beaten	1	box frozen chopped spinach, cooked
1	c. 2% milk		
	Salt and pepper to taste	1	onion, chopped (optional)
	Dash nutmeg		

Preheat oven to 425. Mix together all ingredients and pour into buttered casserole. Set in pan of water. Place into hot oven and lower heat to 350. Bake for about 1 hour and allow to cool so that it may be cut into squares. Serves 4, each 215 calories.
Elizabeth Edwards Killingsworth

Afoot and light-hearted, I take to the open road,
Healthy, free, the world before me,
The long brown path before me,
Leading wherever I choose.
Walt Whitman

Cream of Potato Soup

3 or 4	potatoes (diced)	3/4	tsp. salt
1	onion, finely chopped	3	c. skim milk
6	T. flour		Dash of pepper

Boil potatoes and onion for 10-15 minutes. Melt margarine in saucepan over low heat. Blend in flour, salt, dash of pepper. Add milk all at once, stirring constantly until mixture begins to thicken. Remove from heat and add potatoes and onions. Heat and serve. Garnish with chopped chives, bacon bits and cheese. Serves 4-6, each 172 calories, 0 fat grams. *Helene Murphy*

Try substituting evaporated skim milk in this recipe!

Cajun Potato Salad

2	lbs. small red potatoes	1/2	lb. Precooked smoked
1/2	c. red onion, chopped		kielbasa
1/2	c. green onion, sliced	1	T. Dijon mustard
1/4	c. fresh parsley, minced	2	cloves garlic, minced
6	T. cider vinegar, divided	1/2	tsp. pepper
2	T. olive or vegetable oil	1/4	tsp. cayenne pepper

Cook the potatoes in boiling, salted water for 20 to 30 minutes or until tender. Drain. Rinse with cold water, cool completely. Cut into 1/4" slices, place in a large bowl. Add onions, parsley and 3 tablespoons vinegar, and toss. In a medium skillet, cook sausage in oil for 5-10 minutes or until it begins to brown. Remove and add to potato mixture. To drippings in skillet, add mustard, garlic, pepper, cayenne pepper and remaining vinegar – bring to a boil, whisking constantly. Pour over salad, toss gently. Serve immediately. Serves 6, each 1 1/2 starch, 1 high-fat meat; 210 calories. *Mary Cooper*

New Potato Salad

3	lbs. red skin new potatoes	1	c. plain low-fat yogurt
1/2	c. green onions, thinly sliced	2	T. buttermilk
3/4	tsp. garlic salt, divided	1	c. (4-oz.) crumbled blue
1/4	tsp. fresh ground black		cheese
	pepper		

Cut potatoes into 1/2" pieces. Cook in boiling water to cover for 15-20 minutes or until tender. Drain. Combine potatoes, onions, 1/2 tsp. garlic salt and pepper. Toss gently to combine. Stir together yogurt, buttermilk, blue cheese and remaining 1/4 teaspoon garlic salt. Add to potatoes, toss gently to coat. Cover and chill at least 2 hours. Serves 10, each 166 calories, 7 g. protein, 4 g. fat, 27 g. carbohydrates.
Alice Buske

New Potato and Red Onion Salad

2	lbs. red potatoes	*Lemon Vinaigrette:*	
10	oz. frozen artichoke hearts, defrosted OR	1/4	c. fresh basil, finely chopped
18	oz. canned artichoke hearts, drained and rinsed	1/4	c. fresh lemon juice
		1/4	c. white wine vinegar
2	med. red onions, thinly sliced	2	T. olive oil
	Salt and pepper		Salt
1/2	c. Parmesan cheese, shavings		Freshly ground black pepper

In a large pot of salted water, add potatoes, bring to a boil and cook until tender (15 to 20 minutes). Drain the potatoes and quarter if large. In a large bowl, toss the potatoes with the artichoke hearts, red onions, and vinaigrette. Season to taste with salt and pepper. Sprinkle with the shaved Parmesan before serving. Serves 6, each 168 calories.
Linda McClung

Sweet Potato Salad

3	lg. sweet potatoes, cubed	1	lg. carrot, shredded
1	lg. russet potato, diced	2	lg. eggs, hard-boiled, diced
1	med. Vidalia or Walla Walla (sweet) onion, diced	1	c. mayonnaise-type salad dressing

Place cut potatoes in lightly salted water and simmer until slightly tender. Drain quickly and immediately return to pot and cover with dish towel. Allow to "steam" in their own heat and juice till completely cooled to room temperature. This will produce perfect boiled potatoes (every time!). Once potatoes are cooled to room temperature, mix all ingredients together and chill overnight or at least 4 hours. Do NOT add mayo or mayonnaise-type salad dressing to warm potatoes. Serves 6, each 225 calories, 11 g. fat.
John Gunterman

Make it light! Use low-fat or fat-free salad dressing.

Tomato, Basil and Mozzarella Salad

1	lb. tomatoes, large, very ripe (2-3 tomatoes)	8	basil leaves, fresh
2	oz. Mozzarella cheese, shredded	2	tsp. olive oil
			Dash cracked pepper

Slice tomatoes crosswise into $1/2$-inch thick slices, 4 slices per tomato. Arrange 2-3 slices on each salad plate. Sprinkle the mozzarella on top of each tomato. Cut fresh basil leaves into strips and top each tomato with basil. Drizzle olive oil over the tops and add a dash of pepper. Serves 4, exchange: 1 vegetable , 1 medium-fat meat; 4 g. fat, 5 g. protein, 70 calories.
Mark Hopkins

Zesty Orange Salad

2	oranges, peeled, sliced thin	1	T. cider vinegar
1	small onion, sliced thin	1/8	tsp. chili powder
2	tsp. vegetable oil		Lettuce leaves

Combine all ingredients except lettuce leaves in a bowl. Cover and refrigerate for 2 hours before serving. Toss before serving on lettuce leaves. Serves 2, each 1 fruit and 1 fat exchange; 19 g. carbohydrates, 2 g. protein, 4 g. fat; 117 calories.
Heather Boler

Summer Fruit Salad

2	c. cooked rice, cooled to room temperature	1/2	c. banana slices
1/2	c. strawberries, quartered	1/4	c. pineapple juice
1/2	c. grapes, halved	2	T. plain yogurt
1/2	c. kiwi fruit slices, quartered	1	T. honey
1/2	c. pineapple tidbits		Lettuce leaves

Combine rice and fruits in large bowl. Blend pineapple juice, yogurt, and honey in small bowl; pour over rice mixture. Toss lightly. Serve on lettuce leaves. Serves 4, each 2 g. protein, 0.5 g. fat, 37 g. carbohydrates, 161 calories.
Sally Bordonaro

Dad's Potato Salad

1	lg. onion, finely chopped	5	T. oil
4	lbs. potatoes, boiled	1	sprig fresh parsley, minced
3	T. cider vinegar		Salt and pepper

Cut potatoes to desired size while still warm. Put in bowl with onion. Sprinkle with vinegar. Let sit at room temperature about one hour. Add oil, parsley, salt and pepper. Taste and adjust seasonings if necessary. Serves 10, each 175 calories, 5 g. fat.
John Malik

Stuffed Zucchini

4	med. zucchini	1/4	tsp. salt
3	green onions, sliced		Dash pepper
2	T. olive oil		
1	slice of bread, cubed		
1/4	c. Parmesan cheese, grated		
1	med. tomato, chopped		

Cut zucchini lengthwise in halves. Scoop out pulp, leaving 1/4-inch wall; chop pulp and set aside. Place zucchini shells cut sides down in dish. Cover loosely and microwave on high until crisp tender, about 5 to 6 minutes. Cover and microwave pulp, onions and margarine in a 1 1/2-qt. casserole or bowl on high until tender, about 6 to 7 minutes. Stir in bread cubes, cheese, tomato, salt and pepper. Turn zucchini shell cut sides up, spoon mixture into shells. Cover loosely and microwave on high until hot, 2 to 3 minutes. Serves 8, each 197 calories, 4 g. fat.
Kimberly Francis

Corn and Kidney Bean Salad

Salad:

1	16-oz. can red kidney beans, drained and rinsed
2	c. corn kernels
1	green bell pepper, diced
1	red bell pepper, diced
1	stalk celery, diced
1/2	c. chopped scallions, including some green tops

Dressing:

1/4	c. wine vinegar
1	tsp. lemon juice
2	cloves garlic, minced
1/2	tsp. sugar
	Salt and pepper to taste

In a large glass or stainless steel bowl, combine all the salad ingredients. In a small bowl or jar, combine all the ingredients for the salad dressing. Pour the dressing over the salad and mix thoroughly. Better when prepared one day before serving. Serves 6, each 1/2 meat, 1 vegetable, 1 starch.
Ruth Foliano

Bean Salad

1	lb. fresh green beans, 1" pieces, steamed and cooled	1	lg. red onion, coarsely chopped
1	15-oz. can garbanzo beans	1/2	c. seasoned rice vinegar
1	15-oz. can kidney beans		

Combine all ingredients in a sealed plastic container and shake well. Let sit in fridge overnight. Flavor improves with age. Serves 6, each 2 fat grams.
Patricia Ward

Stuffed Tomatoes

4	lg. firm tomatoes	1/4	c. fresh basil, minced
1 1/2	c. sour dough breadcrumbs	1/4	c. Feta cheese
1/4	c. shallots, minced	1/4	c. olive oil
1 T.	garlic, minced	1/4	c. Parmesan cheese

Cut tomatoes in half, scoop out pulp (reserve for another dish or mince into stuffing). Place upside down to drain.

Stuffing:
Combine all except Parmesan. Spoon into tomatoes, place in baking dish. Sprinkle with Parmesan. Bake at 375 degrees until golden brown (approx. 10 minutes). Serves 4, each 1 vegetable, 1/2 starch, 1/2 lean meat, 1 fat., 275 calories.
Shirley Robertson

There was butter for the market,
There was fruit upon the trees,
There were eggs, potatoes, bacon,
And a tidy lot of cheese.
Edward Dyson

Acorn Squash Baked with Pineapple

1	acorn squash, cut in half	1	T. margarine
2	tsp. margarine		Ground nutmeg
2	tsp. brown sugar	1/4	tsp. salt
3	T. crushed pineapple		

Scoop out and discard squash seeds and fiber. Place squash in a baking dish that has been coated with margarine. Put one teaspoon brown sugar and one teaspoon margarine in each half. Cover and bake in hot oven (400 degrees) for 30 minutes. Scoop cooked squash out of shells. Mash squash and combine with margarine, crushed pineapple, nutmeg and salt, if desired, beating until well blended. Fill squash halves with mixture and sprinkle remaining brown sugar on top. Brown one minute under broiler. Serves 2, each 110 calories.
Jo Ann Biggs

Green Bean, New Potatoes & Ham Salad

3	lbs. new potatoes, quartered	1/3	c. spicy brown mustard
2/3	c. cold water	2	T. red wine vinegar
1	lb. green beans, halved	2	c. ham cubes
3/4	c. fat-free whipped salad dressing	1/2	c. chopped green onions

Place potatoes and water in 3-quart microwavable casserole; cover. Microwave on high for 13 minutes. Stir in beans. Microwave on high 7–13 minutes or until potatoes and beans are tender; drain. Mix dressing, mustard and vinegar in large bowl. Add potatoes, beans and remaining ingredients; mix lightly. Refrigerate until ready to serve. Serves 12, each 225 calories.
Christie Galvin

Black Bean Soup

1	slice bacon	1/2	tsp. cumin
1/2	c. onion, chopped	1/2	tsp. salt
1	c. celery	1/2	tsp. fresh ground pepper
2 1/2	c. black beans, cooked and drained	1	carton fat-free sour cream
			Scallions for garnish
2 1/2	c. water		

Fry bacon over medium heat in small, heavy frying pan, crumble bacon and set aside. Heat bacon drippings over medium heat; sauté onion and celery until tender, stirring occasionally. Puree beans in blender or food processor fitted with steel blade. Stir into vegetables. Mix in crumbled bacon and remaining ingredients, stirring occasionally until soup is hot. Top each mug with a dollop of sour cream and a sprinkling of scallions. Serves 6, each 1 starch, 1/2 fat; 6 g protein, 3 g. fat, 124 calories.
Debbie Holloway

Tex-Mex Corn Soup

1	T. margarine	1	16-oz. whole kernel corn, including liquid
1/2	c. onion, chopped		
1	c. sweet red pepper	1/4	tsp. salt
1	tsp. red pepper flakes	1/4	tsp. ground white pepper, fresh
4	c. chicken broth		
1	17-oz. creamed corn, including liquid		

Melt margarine in a large saucepan; sauté onion and sweet pepper with red pepper flakes until tender, stirring occasionally (about 2 minutes). Stir in chicken broth and both cans of corn. Continue cooking until it is very hot. Add salt and pepper and serve immediately. Serves 8, each 2 starch, 1 fat; 6 g. protein, 8 g. fat, 205 calories.
Melissa Martinez

Fresh Tomato-Basil Soup

2   t. olive oil
1   c. onions, chopped
1/2   garlic clove, mashed
6   lg. plum tomatoes, blanched, peeled, seeded and chopped

1   c. low-sodium chicken broth
2   T. fresh basil, chopped + 2 sprigs basil

Heat oil in a 1 1/2 qt. nonstick saucepan. Add onions and garlic. Cook over medium-high heat until crisp-tender, about two minutes. Stir in remaining ingredients and bring to a boil. Reduce heat to low and simmer, stirring occasionally, until flavors blend, about 15 minutes. Pour into bowls and garnish with sprigs of basil. Serves 2, each 114 calories, 6 g. fat.
Marge Schilling

Cheese Tomato

1   tomato, thickly sliced
1   dash celery salt
1   dash garlic salt

1   dash pepper
1   oz. American cheese, grated

Place tomato slices on broiler pan coated with vegetable cooking spray. Sprinkle with seasonings. Top with cheese. Broil 5-6 inches from heat until cheese is melted. Serves 1, 1 vegetable, 1 high-fat meat, 140 calories.
Al Bordonaro

Corn Casserole

1   15-oz. can creamed corn
1   15-oz. can undrained, whole-kernel corn
2   T. sugar

2   eggs, slightly beaten
1/3   c. cornbread mix
4   T. butter or low-fat margarine, softened

Coat a 9-inch glass pie plate with nonstick spray. In a large bowl, combine corn, sugar, eggs, cornbread mix and butter and mix well. Pour batter into plate and bake one hour in a 350 degree oven; knife when inserted should come out clean. Serves 6, each 1 meat, 2 bread, 1 fat; 295 calories.
Mary Cooper

Pasta and Vegetable Toss

2	t. olive oil	1½	c. cooked rotini (spiral) pasta
1	c. onions, sliced		
1	c. zucchini, shredded	1	T. fresh Italian parsley, chopped
1	c. carrots, shredded		
1	clove garlic, minced	2	t. balsamic or red wine vinegar

In 9-inch non-stick skillet, heat oil. Add onions, zucchini, carrots and garlic. Cook over medium heat, stirring occasionally until onions are tender, about 5 minutes. Add macaroni to skillet and stir to combine. Add parsley and vinegar and stir. Reduce heat to low and cook, stirring frequently, until thoroughly heated, about one minute. Serves 8, each 219 calories, 5 g. fat.
Marge Schilling

Tomatoes Oregano

6	large, ripe tomatoes		Worcestershire sauce to taste
	Sprinkle of oregano	1	c. soft breadcrumbs
	Garlic salt to taste	1	T. olive oil
	Black pepper to taste		Sprinkle of Parmesan cheese

Cut tomatoes in half. Place cut side up in a baking dish. Sprinkle with oregano,, garlic salt and pepper. Moisten breadcrumbs in Worcestershire sauce and oil. Top each tomato with crumbs, then sprinkle with cheese. Bake at 350 for 25-30 minutes. Serves 12, each 60 calories.
Frances Hixon

A world without tomatoes
Is like a string quartet without violins.
Laurie Colwin

Asparagus Vinaigrette

18	spears fresh asparagus	2	t. olive oil
1/4	c. canned low-sodium chicken broth	1/2	t. grated orange peel Pepper to taste
2	T. raspberry or rice vinegar		

In one-quart shallow microwavable casserole, arrange asparagus spears. Add broth and cover. Microwave on high for 2½ minutes, rotating casserole ½ turn after one minute. Add remaining ingredients, cover and microwave on high 30 seconds, until asparagus is crisp-tender. Delicious cold, also! Serves 3, ea. 76 calories, 5 g. fat.
Marge Schilling

Cranberry Salad

½	c. red currant jelly	1	can cranberry sauce
⅓	c. orange marmalade		

Mix all together! Refrigerate. Serves 4, each 25 calories.
Joan Becker

Jezebel Sauce

1	lg. jar pineapple preserves	¾	jar of horseradish
1	lg. jar apple jelly	¾	small can of dry mustard

Mix all ingredients together and heat until blended. Serve hot or cold on ham, beef, lamb, or other meats. This will keep indefinitely in covered container in refrigerator. Usually served at room temperature.
Nadine Larsen

Oven French Fries

4   medium potatoes   Parmesan cheese
1   T. oil

Peel potatoes and cut into long strips, about 1/2" wide. Dry strips
thoroughly on paper towels. Toss in a bowl with oil as if making a salad.
When strips are thoroughly coated with the oil, spread them in a single
layer on a cookie sheet and place in 475 degree oven for 35 minutes.
Turn strips periodically to brown on all sides. If a crisper, browner potato
is desired, place under broiler for a minute or two. Variation: Use
scrubbed unpeeled potatoes. Sprinkle with 2 tablespoons Parmesan
cheese during last 10 minutes. Serves 6, each 80 calories.
Sharon Christopher

For more nutritional value (and less work!), leave the peel on the potatoes.

Baked Cauliflower Casserole

4   c. cauliflower florets,   1 1/2 oz. mozzarella cheese,
     blanched   shredded
1/2 c. tomato sauce   2   T. Parmesan, cheese, grated

Preheat oven to 375. Spray a 9-inch glass pie plate with non-stick spray.
Arrange cauliflower in pie plate and spoon tomato sauce over cauliflower.
In a small mixing bowl, combine cheeses and sprinkle over tomato sauce.
Bake until cauliflower is thoroughly heated, about 15 minutes. Serves 4,
each 74 calories, 3 g. fat.
Marge Schilling

It's all right to drink like a fish –
If you drink what a fish drinks!
Mary Pettibose Poole

Garden Soup

6	c. water	1/2	c. carrots, sliced
2	c. tomato juice	1/2	c. celery, chopped
1	c. potato, peeled and chopped	2	T. chicken bouillon granules; flavored
1	c. onion, chopped	1	tsp. garlic powder
1 c.	lima beans	1 1/2	tsp. Worcestershire sauce
3/4	c. chicken, cooked, chopped		

Combine all ingredients in a large Dutch oven. Cover and bring to a boil. Reduce heat and simmer 45 minutes to 1 hour. Serve hot. Serves 10, each 1 starch exchange, 84 calories, 15 g. carbohydrates, 4 g. protein, 1 g. fat.
Frances Hixon

Roasted Poblano Pepper Soup

3	Poblano peppers, roasted, de-seeded and cut into strips	3	c. chicken stock
		1	8-oz. cream cheese, cubed
3	onions, chopped and sautéed in butter	1	8-oz. sour cream

Saute onions in chicken stock. Add cubed cream cheese. Add sour cream and poblanos. Put all ingredients into a blender and mix well. Optional: add diced, cooked chicken or corn. Serve hot or cold. Serves 2, each 195 calories.
Nina Dahlstrom Stowers

Make it light! Use low-fat cream cheese and sour cream.

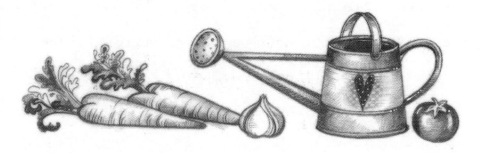

Top 10 Most Healing Foods

These foods are loaded with antioxidants, the natural enemies of dangerous particles called free radicals. Free radicals can alter your DNA in ways that cause cancer, or change LDL cholesterol so it sticks to artery walls, impeding circulation. Fight back by consuming super-nutritional foods that neutralize free radicals.

1. The number one source of antioxidants is…. **BLUEBERRIES!** According to the USDA Human Nutrition Research Center on Aging at Tufts University, blueberries beat out all the other fruits and veggies with their antioxidant power. It comes from antho-cyanin pigments that give blueberries their deep blue color. So, sprinkle some over your cereal, stir some into your smoothie, scatter them over your sherbet or blend them into pancakes…find a way to welcome blueberries into your life! OTHER BERRIES, such as strawberries, blackberries, and raspberries, all contain fiber, vitamin C, and ellagic acid, an antioxidant that helps prevent cataracts, cancer and constipation. Eat them raw to protect the vitamin C.

The remaining nine healing foods are:

2. **BEANS** – Black-eyed peas, chickpeas, kidney beans and lima beans are chock-full of fiber and antioxidants, and can help lower cholesterol, stabilize your blood sugar and reduce your risk of breast cancer.

3. **BROCCOLI** – Contains two powerful cancer-fighting compounds, plus fiber and beta-carotene, which helps prevent heart disease, cataracts and certain cancers.

4. **CARROTS** – Contain rich amounts of beta-carotene, which helps improve night vision and protects against heart disease, cancer and macular degeneration. Lightly cooking carrots helps release the beta-carotene.

(continued on next page)

(continued)

5. **FISH** – Salmon, mackerel, rainbow trout, albacore tuna, whitefish, caviar and sardines contain omega-3 fatty acids to help prevent heart disease.

6. **MILK** – Has the power to help strengthen bones, prevent osteoporosis, and lower blood pressure and cholesterol… stick with skim or 1% milk to lower fat and calories.

7. **NUTS** – Almonds, walnuts and peanuts (though really a bean) are good choices that contain antioxidants called flavonoids that protect against heart disease and help lower cholesterol. Walnuts contain those good omega-3 fats, too. Sprinkle nuts on cereals or salads to control portions, as nuts are high in calories.

8. **ONIONS** – Contain compounds that lower cholesterol, thin the blood and prevent hardening of the arteries.

9. **ORANGES** – Aid healing, boost immunity, and help the body absorb iron with their rich content of vitamin C. The pectin in oranges also helps lower cholesterol and control blood sugar. Most of the pectin is in the white layer just beneath the skin, so eat that too!

10. **TOMATOES** – Are rich in two antioxidants, lycopene and vitamin C, which protect against heart disease and some cancers. The ripest tomatoes, besides tasting the best, are the best for you. Cook them in a little oil for better absorption of nutrients. You can also get lycopene from tomato paste and spaghetti sauce.

It's all about CHOICES!

Instead of...	Choose...
Bacon	Canadian bacon
Buttered bread	Crusty bread dipped in olive oil
Gooeycheese	Feta, Parmesan, low-fat cottage cheese, ricotta, or part-skim mozzarella
Fried Chicken	Skinless baked, broiled or grilled chicken
Baking chocolate, 1 oz.	3 T. unsweetened cocoa plus 1 tsp. vegetable oil
Baked potato, loaded	Baked potato with chicken broth or salsa and veggies
Corn chips	Baked tortilla chips
Cream sauce or gravy	Clear broth
Croissant	Bagel
Doughnut	Angel food cake
Evaporated condensed milk	Skim evaporated condensed milk
French fries	Baked oven fries
Ground beef	Ground turkey
Ice cream	Frozen non-fat ice cream, yogurt or sorbet
Mayonnaise	Light or nonfat mayonnaise
Milk, whole	Skim or low-fat milk
Popcorn with butter	Popcorn with garlic powder or chili powder
Potato chips	Pretzels
Sour cream	Low-fat sour cream or yogurt, or low-fat cottage cheese, blended until smooth
Tuna in oil	Tuna in spring water
Whipped cream	Low-fat whipped topping or nonfat vanilla yogurt

Desserts

Heavenly Sweets & Luscious

Very Light Strawberry Delight

1/4	c. chopped pecans	2	tsp. fresh lemon juice
16	reduced-fat vanilla wafers, crushed	2	T. honey
1	pint fresh strawberries or 1 (10-oz.) package, frozen	1	12-oz. tub frozen fat-free whipped topping, thawed

Place the chopped pecans on a baking sheet and toast until lightly golden and fragrant, about 7 minutes. Combine toasted pecans and vanilla wafers and mix well. Set aside. Thaw the frozen berries, or slice fresh berries and place in a large bowl. Add the lemon juice and honey and blend with a hand mixer until strawberries are pureed (or use a blender). Set aside. Fold together the strawberry puree and the whipped topping. Try not to stir too much as the air will be released from the topping. Lightly fold the mixtures together with a rubber spatula until most of the streaks are blended in to make a nice pink color. Place 2/3 cup of the vanilla wafer crumbs and nuts into the bottom of a 9-inch square pan and spread evenly. Spoon the strawberry mixture over it and smooth the top. Sprinkle with the remaining 1/3 of crumbs, cover tightly and place in freezer until firm. Serves 8, each 45 calories, 2 g. fat, 1 g. protein, 33 g. carbohydrates.
Ruth Foliano

Refreshing Frozen Fruit Salad

1	small pkg. strawberry gelatin	1	small can Mandarin oranges
1	c. water, boiling	3/4	c. seedless green grapes
6	oz. pink lemonade concentrate	1	small jar maraschino cherries (reserve some for garnish)
8	oz. prepared whipped topping, thawed	2	bananas, sliced 1/4" thick

In large bowl, dissolve gelatin in boiling water; add lemonade concentrate and stir until melted. Chill until slightly thickened, about 45 minutes. Blend in whipped topping; fold in fruit. Pour into 9" x 5" loaf pan. Freeze about 4 hours or until firm. Turn out onto a serving plate. Garnish with additional whipped topping and cherries if desired. Serves 6, each 45 calories.
A Volunteer

Forgotten Cookies

2	egg whites			Pinch of salt
1	tsp. vanilla		1	c. chocolate or butterscotch
3/4	c. sugar			chips
1	c. of chopped pecans			

Preheat oven at 350 degrees; beat egg whites and salt until stiff. Add sugar and beat until peaks form. Add vanilla. Stir in pecans and chips. Drop mixture by teaspoon on greased cookie sheet. Place in oven and turn oven off. Leave overnight or all day until oven has completely cooled. Makes 12, each 55 calories.
Bill Speary

Crazy Crust Apple Squares

1	c. all purpose flour	1/2	c. raisins	
1/2	c. sugar	3	c. (3medium) sliced, peeled	
1	tsp. baking powder		apples	
1/2	tsp. salt	1/2	c. chopped pecans	
1/4	tsp. nutmeg	1/3	c. sugar	
2/3	c. 2% milk	1	tsp. cinnamon	
1	egg			

Grease 13 x 9 inch pan. In large bowl, combine flour, 1/2 cup sugar, baking powder, salt and nutmeg; mix well; add milk and egg, blend well. Spread batter in greased pan. Sprinkle raisins, apples and pecans over batter. In small bowl combine sugar and cinnamon; mix well. Sprinkle sugar mixture over top; Bake at 350 degrees for 30 to 40 minutes or until edges are golden brown and apples are tender. Makes 12, each 95 calories, 4 g. fat.
Janice Andreas

Had I but one penny in the world,
thou should have it for gingerbread.
William Shakespeare

Vivian's Quick Snack Cookies

½	c. sugar	1	c. creamy peanut butter
½	c. white corn syrup	2	c. crisp rice cereal

Place sugar and syrup in a saucepan and bring just to a boil (do not boil); when mixture is hot, quickly add and mix in 1 cup of creamy peanut butter and 2 cups cereal. Drop by teaspoonfuls onto waxed paper. Let these little cookies cool a bit before indulging. Makes 1 dozen, each 45 calories, 8 g. fat.
Pat Walker

Chocolate Éclair Icebox Dessert

1	14-oz. box low-fat honey graham crackers	8	oz. tub fat-free whipped topping
	Cooking spray	2	T. oleo, softened, not melted
3	c. skim milk	2	T. honey
2	3.4 oz. pkgs. fat-free vanilla pudding mix	2	oz. unsweetened chocolate, melted
8	oz. tub fat-free cream cheese	1½	c. powdered sugar
¼	c. skim milk		

Arrange graham crackers in the bottom of a 13x9″ baking dish coated with cooking spray. Combine 3 cups milk, pudding mix, and cream cheese in a large bowl, and beat at low speed of mixer, for one minute or until thick. Fold in whipped topping. Spread half of the pudding mixture over graham crackers and top with graham crackers. Repeat the procedure with the remaining half of the pudding mixture and graham crackers. Combine ¼ cup milk, softened oleo, honey, and unsweetened chocolate in a medium bowl, and beat well with a mixer. Gradually add powdered sugar to milk mixture, and beat well. Spread chocolate glaze over graham crackers. Cover dessert by making a tent with foil; chill 4 hours. Makes 18 servings, each 98 calories, 17 g. carbohydrates, 2 g. fat.
Dorothy Hoban

Chocolate Peanut Puffs

1/4	c. honey	12	oz. jar peanut butter
1/2	c. white karo syrup		(crunchy)
1	c. sugar	4	c. chocolate puff cereal

Combine honey, syrup and sugar; bring to a boil; add peanut butter; stir well and pour over cocoa puffs. Drop cookies on to wax paper. Makes 2 dozen, each 55 calories, 3 g. fat.
Elma Hinojosa

Quick Peanut Butter Squares

1	c. sugar	5	c. crisp rice cereal
1	c. white corn syrup	1	c. chocolate chips
1	c. peanut butter	1	c. butterscotch chips

Melt sugar and syrup in large pan. Bring to a good boil; remove from burner and add peanut butter and stir well; add rice cereal to mixture and stir well. Pour into buttered 9 x 13 inch pan. Melt chips in microwave and spread on top. Refrigerate. Makes 36 servings, each 70 calories, 8 g. fat.
Pat Yates

Easy Lemon Bars

1	box "one-step" angel food cake mix	1	can lemon pie filling

Mix together, pour into shallow cookie sheet; bake at 350 degrees for 15 to 20 minutes. Makes 36 bars, each 95 calories, 5 g. fat.
Viola Van Houten

> *Thank you for the world so sweet,*
> *Thank you for the food we eat*
> *Thank you for the birds that sing,*
> *Thank you, God, for everything.*

Stone Jar Cookies

1	c. vegetable shortening	2	eggs (well beaten)
1	tsp. salt	3	c. flour
1	tsp. vanilla	1	tsp. baking soda
1	tsp. nutmeg	1/4	c. milk
1	c. brown sugar	1	c. pecans (chopped)

Mix in order and drop on greased cookie sheet; bake at 350 degrees for 30 minutes. Makes 5 dozen, each 65 calories, 7 g. carbohydrates, 4 g. fat.
Ella H. Nicolas

Easy One-Bowl Sugar Cookies

2	eggs	3/4	c. sugar
2/3	c. canola oil	2	c. flour
2	tsp. vanilla	2	tsp. baking powder
1	tsp. grated lemon rind	1/4	tsp. salt

Preheat oven to 400 degrees. Beat eggs with fork; stir in oil, vanilla and rind; blend in sugar until mixture thickens; add flour, baking powder and salt and stir into egg mixture until blended. Drop by teaspoon, 2 inches apart, on an ungreased baking sheet; bake 8 to 10 minutes; remove from sheet and allow to cool on rack. Makes about 3 dozen, each cookie 35 calories, 2 g. fat.
Rita Utley Gonzales

Chocolate Fudge Cookies

2	cans condensed milk	1	tsp. vanilla
2	c. flour	1 1/2	c. pecans, chopped
3/4	stick soft margarine		
4	c. chocolate chips, divided		

Mix milk and flour. Combine 3 cups chocolate chips and oleo. Mix flour mixture with chocolate mixture. Stir in remaining chocolate chips, vanilla and nuts. Drop by tablespoonfuls on greased cookie sheet. Bake at 325 degrees for 8 to 10 minutes; they are soft when done; remove from cookie sheet immediately. Makes about 4 dozen, each cookie 95 calories, 9 g. fat.
Elizabeth Edwards Killingsworth

Chunky Oatmeal Cookies

1	c. white sugar	1	tsp. baking powder
1	c. brown sugar, packed	1	c. crushed corn flakes
1	c. butter, melted	1¼	c. oatmeal
2	eggs	½	c. chocolate chips
1	tsp. vanilla	½	c. pecans, broken
2	c. flour	½	c. raisins
1	tsp. baking soda		

Mix sugars, melted butter, eggs and vanilla. Sift dry ingredients together and add to creamed mixture. In another bowl mix corn flake crumbs, oatmeal, chocolate chips, pecans and raisins. Combine with creamed mixture. Drop from teaspoons onto greased cookie sheet. Bake at 350 for 8 to 10 minutes. Makes 72 cookies, each 97 calories, 1 g. protein, 24 g. carbohydrates, 5 g. fat.
Marguerite J. Ross

Crisp Rice Cookies

2	egg whites	½	tsp. vanilla
¼	tsp. salt	3 c.	crisp rice cereal
¾	c. sugar		

Beat egg whites and salt until almost stiff; add vanilla; add sugar gradually, beating after each addition; fold in cereal. Drop by level measuring tablespoonfuls onto well greased cookie sheet. Bake at 325 degrees for about 12 to 15 minutes; remove from pan immediately. Makes about 3 dozen 2-inch cookies, each 25 calories, 0 g. fat.
Marguerite J. Ross

Party Cookies

Fat-free vanilla or chocolate wafers
Prepared whipped topping
Multicolored sprinkles or bits of cut fruit

Place 1 tsp. topping on each wafer and decorate with fruit or sprinkles. Up to 3 cookies is less than ½ carbohydrate – therefore free.
Cherl Jay

Pineapple Cookies

2	c. sifted flour	1	egg
1	tsp. baking powder	1/2	tsp. vanilla
1	tsp. salt	1/2	c. drained crushed pineapple
1/2	c. soft shortening	1/4	tsp. nutmeg (optional)
1	c. sugar	1	tsp. granulated sugar

Mix shortening, sugar and egg until creamy. Add pineapple, then dry ingredients.
Drop on cookie sheet; sprinkle with nutmeg and sugar. Bake at 375 degrees for
about 12 minutes. Makes about 3 dozen, each cookie 65 calories, 1 g. protein, 7
g. carbohydrates, 4 g. fat, 4 mg. cholesterol; 49 mg. sodium.
Ruth M. Botello

Chocolate Chocolate-Chip Cookies

3/4	c. vegetable oil	1 1/2	c. all-purpose flour
2/3	c. sugar	1/3	c. unsweetened cocoa
1	egg	1/4	c. walnuts, chopped
1	t. baking powder	1/2	c. semi-sweet chocolate
1/2	t. baking soda		chips

Beat together oil, sugar and egg. Add the remaining ingredients and stir to
blend well. Let stand for 10 minutes. Drop by spoonfuls about one inch apart
onto a lightly oiled baking sheet. Bake 8 to 10 minutes at 375. Makes 36,
each 106 calories, 2 g. protein, 18 g. carbohydrates, 6 g. fat, 124 mg. sodium,
1 starch exchange.
Patricia Ward

Oatmeal Cookies

2	c. rolled oats	1	tsp. baking soda
1	c. packed brown sugar	1/4	c. hot water
1/2	c. sugar	1/2	c. shortening, melted and
1	c. all purpose flour		cooled
1/4	tsp. salt	1	tsp. vanilla

In mixing bowl, combine oats, sugars, flour and salt; combine soda and
water; stir into oats mixture along with shortening and vanilla. Roll into
walnut size balls; place on greased cooking sheet; bake at 350 degrees for
about 10 minutes or until golden brown; remove from oven; allow to
stand 2 minutes before removing to wire rack to cool. Makes about 3 1/2
dozen, each 75 calories, 13 g. carbohydrates, 5 g. fat.
Ofelia M. Alaniz

Wonderful Peanut Butter Cookies

¹/₄	c. vegetable oil	1¹/₂	c. flour
¹/₂	c. peanut butter, smooth or chunky	¹/₂	t. baking powder
		³/₄	t. baking soda
¹/₂	c. dark brown sugar	¹/₄	c. water
1	egg		

Mix oil, peanut butter, sugar and egg. Stir in the remaining ingredients. Chill dough for three hours or overnight. Roll into walnut-sized balls. Place on lightly greased baking sheet. Flatten with a fork. Bake at 375 for 10 to 12 minutes. Makes 36, 61 calories each.
Arnetta Autrey

Yummy Nuggets

4 to 6 oz.	butterscotch morsels	1	12 oz. can roasted Spanish peanuts
1	5 oz. can crisp Chinese noodles		

Melt morsels in a heavy pot or double boiler. Mix in noodles and nuts. Drop on wax paper using a teaspoon. Cool until firm. Store in an airtight container. Makes 12-15 cookies, each 45 calories, 5 g. fat.
Anna Mae Edwards

Snickerdoodles

1	c. soft margarine	2	tsp. cream of tartar
1¹/₂	c. sugar	1	tsp. baking soda
2	eggs	¹/₂	tsp. salt
2³/₄	c. flour		

Mix the margarine, sugar and eggs. Stir in flour, cream of tartar, soda and salt. Chill dough; roll into balls the size of walnuts. Mix together 2 tablespoons of sugar and 2 teaspoons of cinnamon; roll ball into mixture and place on greased cookie sheet at 400 degrees for 18-20 minutes, till brown but soft. Make 3 dozen, each 136 calories, 23 mg cholesterol, 4 g. fat.
Sue Wilsey

Applesauce Bar Cookies

1³/₄	c. sifted cake flour	¹/₄	c. margarine
¹/₂	t. baking soda	³/₄	c. sugar
1	t. cinnamon	1	egg
¹/₂	t. allspice	¹/₂	c. unsweetened applesauce
¹/₈	t. cloves	¹/₂	c. raisins
¹/₂	t. salt		

Preheat oven to 375 degrees. Prepare bottom of a 11 x 7 inch pan with non-stick coating. Sift together flour, baking soda, spices and salt. Cream together margarine and sugar. Add egg to margarine mixture and beat until light and fluffy. Alternately add the dry ingredients and applesauce, stirring just enough to blend. Fold in the raisins. Turn into the prepared pan and bake about 30 minutes. Let cool for 15 minutes, then cut into 24 squares. Each, 2 g. fat, 15 g. carbohydrates, 80 calories, 1 bread and ¹/₂ fat exchange.
JoAnn

Hawaiian Delight

1	small pkg. lemon gelatin	1	3 oz. pkg. cream cheese, softened
1	small pkg. lime gelatin		
1	c. boiling water	1	8-oz. container whipped topping
1	small can crushed pineapple		
¹/₂	c. chopped pecans		

Put gelatin into serving container, add boiling water and mix at low speed until it is dissolved. Add cream cheese and mix at low speed until mixture is smooth. Stir in pineapple with juice until mixture is well combined. Stir in pecans, then add whipped topping and stir, slowly, until topping is blended with other ingredients. Refrigerate 4 hours before serving. Serves 8, each 75 calories, 5 g. fat.
Joanne Thompson

Make it light! Choose fat-free cream cheese and whipped topping.

Chocolate Mint Squares

1	c. evaporated skim milk	1¹/₂	c. granulated sugar
³/₄	c. unsweetened cocoa powder	¹/₂	t. baking powder
		¹/₂	t. baking soda
1	c. unsweetened applesauce	¹/₂	t. salt
1	T. pure vanilla extract		Whites from 4 eggs, at room
2	c. all-purpose flour		temperature

Topping:

1	Envelope powdered whipped topping mix	2	c. confectioners' sugar
		2	t. peppermint extract.
3	T. evaporated skim milk		

Heat oven to 350 degrees and grease a 13x9-inch baking pan. In a medium saucepan, heat evaporated milk until barely simmering. Remove from heat and whisk in the cocoa until thickened. Let stand 2 or 3 minutes to cool slightly. Whisk in the applesauce and vanilla. In a large bowl, mix flour, 1 1/4 cups of granulated sugar, baking powder, baking soda and salt. In a medium bowl, beat egg whites with an electric mixer until thick and foamy. Gradually beat in remaining 1/4 c. of granulated sugar until stiff peaks form when beaters are lifted. Pour cocoa mixture over the flour and stir to blend. With a spatula, gently stir 1/4 of the egg whites into the flour, Gently fold in the remaining egg whites until no white streaks remain. Pour the batter in the baking pan. Bake for 25 to 30 minutes, or until a toothpick comes out clean. Set pan on a wire rack to cool. To make topping, beat the topping mix and evaporated milk on low speed until smooth. Beat in confectioners' sugar and peppermint extract, gradually increasing mixer speed to high, until frosting is thick and smooth. Spread frosting over top of cake. Let set until firm before cutting into squares. Makes 24 squares, each 162 calories, 3 g. protein, 36 g. carbohydrates, 1 g. fat.
Cardiac Rehab, CHRISTUS Schumpert

> Lord help me today
> to remember the difference one makes.
> One smile, one compliment, one helping hand,
> Doing one thing someone else can't do.
> Lord help me today to be more like you. Amen

Coffee Shop Fudge

1	c. chopped pecans	2	T. strong brewed coffee,
3	c. (18 oz.) semisweet		room temperature
	chocolate chips	1	tsp. ground cinnamon
1	can (14 oz.) sweetened	1/8	tsp. salt
	condensed milk	1	tsp. vanilla extract

Line an 8-inch square pan with foil and butter the foil; set aside. Place pecans in microwave safe plate; microwave, uncovered, on high for 4 minutes, stirring after each minute, set aside. In a 2-quart microwave safe bowl, combine chocolate chips, milk, coffee, cinnamon and salt. Microwave, uncovered, on high for 1 1/2 minutes. Stir until smooth. Stir in vanilla and pecans. Immediately spread into the prepared pan; cover and refrigerate until firm, about 2 hours; remove from pan; cut into 1 inch squares; cover and store at room temperature. Makes 2 pounds. Each square, 72 calories, 10 g. carbohydrates, 7 g. fat.
Pat Walker

Low-Fat Rocky Road Brownies

4	egg whites, beaten	1/2	t. baking powder
1/2	c. sugar	1/4	t. salt
1	T. vanilla extract	1/2	c. flour
1/2	c. unsweetened cocoa	1	c. marshmallow cream
	powder		

Prepare a 9 x 13 pan with cooking spray and flour. In a large bowl, combine baking powder, cocoa, salt and flour. Beat egg whites. Add to egg whites sugar, vanilla and marshmallow cream. Mix dry ingredients with wet ingredients and bake at 325 for 18 minutes. Serves 8, each 0 g. fat.
Lisa Stansbury

Creamy Rice Pudding

1/2	c. short grain rice			Nutmeg to taste
1	c. boiling water		1/2	c. raisins
1/3	c. sugar		2	egg yolks
1	tsp. cornstarch		1	tsp. pure vanilla
1/4	tsp. salt		2	T. butter
4	c. milk		1	T. cinnamon (to garnish)
1	c. cream (10%)			

Combine the rice with the boiling water in a medium sized saucepan;
cover; simmer gently 15 minutes or until the water is absorbed.
Combine the sugar with the cornstarch and salt; whisk in 1 cup milk. Add
sugar mixture, along with the remaining milk and cream, to the saucepan
with the rice. Add the nutmeg and the raisins; stir to a boil, reduce heat;
simmer 1 hour or until creamy. Remove from the heat, quickly whisk in
the egg yolks, the vanilla and butter. Serve hot or cold, garnish with
cinnamon. Serves 4, each 275 calories, 13 g. fat.
Joanne Thompson

Escalloped Pineapple

5	slices cubed bread (either white or dark)		1	c. sugar
			1	can pineapple tidbits (20 oz.), undrained
3	eggs			
1/2	tsp. salt		1/2	c. melted butter

Beat eggs and sugar together; add other ingredients and mix well; pour
into 9x13 inch pan and bake for 30 minutes at 350 degrees. Makes 8
servings, each 195 calories, 11 g. fat.
Phyllis Kannowski

Goodness is the only investment that never fails.
Henry David Thoreau

Chocolate Marshmallow Pie

1	milk chocolate candy bar with almonds (7 oz.)	1/2	c. milk
16	large marshmallows	2	c. whipping cream, whipped
		1	chocolate crumb crust

Place candy bar, marshmallows and milk in heavy saucepan; cook over low heat, stirring constantly until chocolate is melted and mixture is smooth; cool. Fold in whipped cream, pour into crust. Refrigerate for at least 3 hours. Serves 8, each 415 calories.
Vi Teel

Key Lime Pie

1	graham cracker crust	1/2	c. freshly squeezed lime juice
1	can (14 oz.) sweetened condensed milk	1	tsp. grated lime rind
1 1/4	c. sour cream	1	T. sugar

Mix condensed milk, 1/2 cup sour cream, lime juice and grated lime rind; pour filling into crust; refrigerate until firm. Stir 3/4 cup sour cream with sugar; carefully spread over top of pie filling; chill. Before serving, garnish with thin slices of lime. Makes 8 servings, each 410 calories.
Gale Yast

Make it light! Use fat-free sweetened condensed milk and sour cream.

Lemon Icebox Pie

1	14-oz. can sweetened condensed milk	1	12-oz. container of prepared whipped topping
1	6-oz. frozen lemonade concentrate	1	8 or 9 inch graham cracker pie crust

In large bowl, mix milk, concentrate and whipped topping; pour into crust and freeze. 8 servings, each 315 calories, 9 g. fat.
Brian Watson

No Added Sugar Apple Pie

4	c. apples, peeled and sliced	2	t. tapioca or cornstarch
1/2	c. frozen apple juice concentrate, undiluted	1	t. cinnamon
			Pastry shell

Mix apples and remaining ingredients until well coated. Pour into pastry shell and bake at 425 degrees for 40 to 45 minutes.
A Volunteer

Banana Caramel Pie

1	9-inch baked pastry shell	3	chocolate-toffee candy bars, frozen and crushed
1	can condensed milk		
2	large bananas		Small container prepared whipped topping

Place unopened can of condensed milk with label removed, in heavy pot; cover with water and simmer 3 to 4 hours, replenishing water when necessary; remove can, let cool thoroughly. Line bottom of pie shell with bananas and cooked milk (milk will be very thick and brown and taste like caramel); spoon and spread over bananas. Top with cool whip and crushed candy crumbs. Refrigerate until set. Serves 6, each 275 calories.
Elizabeth Edwards Killingsworth

Healthier Chocolate Banana Cream Pie

6	T. peanut butter	1	small package sugar-free chocolate pudding mix
1	T. honey		
2	c. crisp rice cereal	2 1/4	c. 2% milk
2	bananas	1	tub low-fat whipped topping

Mix peanut butter with honey; then mix in cereal. Press in pie plate with metal spoon, building up the edge. Slice banana over crust, then mix pudding with milk and spread over bananas. Top with whipped topping. Only trace amounts of sugar; 3 g. fat.
Joan Becker

Pumpkin Pie

1	16-oz. can solid pack pumpkin	1/2	c. biscuit mix
1	13-oz can evaporated skim milk	4	tsp. sugar
		8	packets sugar substitute (recommended for baking)
1	large egg	2	tsp. pumpkin pie spice
2	egg whites	1	tsp. vanilla

Preheat oven to 350 degrees. Spray a 9-inch pie pan with nonstick cooking spray. Place all ingredients in blender, food processor or mixing bowl. Blend one minute, or beat two minutes with mixer. Pour into pie pan and bake for 50 minutes or until center is puffed up. To serve, cut into eight equal pieces. Each serving, 1^1/$_2$ carbohydrates.
Cheryl Jay

Little Apricot Pies

8 or 9 tortillas
1   large can of apricot pie filling
     (substitute with apple, peach,
     cherry, etc.)

Butter
Brown or white sugar and
cinnamon to taste

Use an oblong baking pan to accommodate 8 or 9 rolled up flour tortillas; spray pan with cooking spray. Heat oven to 350 degrees; lightly butter both sides of tortillas; this will make them crispy and lightly browned on the outside, sort of like pie crust. Spoon about two tablespoons of the pie filling down the center of each tortilla. Loosely roll up each tortilla (like an enchilada) and place the seam side down in pan (some of the filling will run out, it will be ok). Sprinkle the rolled up tortillas with sugar and cinnamon. Bake until hot and bubbly and slightly browned. Take out of the oven, and with a sharp knife, cut down the middle of each tortilla, which will then make 16 delicious rolled-up servings. Ice cream on top is always a plus. Each 175 calories, 7 g. fat.
Pat Walker

Fresh Strawberry Pie

3   pkgs. sugar substitute
1   small box sugar-free
     strawberry gelatin
3   c. fresh (or frozen)
     strawberries, sliced
3   T. cornstarch

1   c. hot water
1   baked pie crust (see bran
     cereal crust, below)
1   tub prepared low-fat
     whipped topping

Mix gelatin, cornstarch and hot water and cook over medium heat about a minute. Add sugar substitute and let cool. Add strawberries to gelatin mixture to coat. Pour into pie shell and refrigerate. Top with whipped topping before serving. Serves 8, each 3/4 bread, 1/2 fruit, 1 fat exchange; 0 cholesterol, 8 g. carbohydrates, 1 g. fat, 1 g. protein, 1 g. fiber, 26 mg. sodium, and 49 calories.
Becky Waggoner

Yummy Strawberry Pie

3	c. sliced strawberries	1	box sugar free strawberry
1³/₄	c. water		gelatin
6	tsp. cornstarch		Optional – 1 piecrust –
3	packages sugar substitute		baked
	(for baking)		Prepared whipped topping

Mix cornstarch and water on medium heat until mixture gets thick. Add gelatin and sugar substitute. Let cool before you add strawberries. Pour into baked pie shell. Let stand 30 minutes. Add topping and serve. (*Hint:* for a "free" dessert, spray pan with nonstick cooking spray and delete the crust.) Serves 8, each 1 carbohydrate and 1 fat.
Cheryl Jay

Perfect Pie Crust

4	c. flour	1	large egg
3	T. sugar	¹/₂	c. water
¹/₂	tsp. salt	2	T. vinegar
1³/₄	c. shortening		

In a large bowl add flour, sugar, salt and shortening. In a smaller bowl mix egg, water and vinegar. Combine the 2 mixtures; divide into 5 parts and refrigerate; will keep for 2 weeks in refrigerator, or it can be frozen. (Food values will depend on filling.)
Elizabeth Edwards Killingsworth

Bran Pie Crust

1	cup all bran cereal	2	T. diet margarine, melted
4	T. flour	¹/₂	c. apple juice

Combine all ingredients. Press into pan sprayed with non-stick cooking spray. Bake at 375 degrees for 12 minutes. Allow to cool. For 8-slice pie, each 1 bread, ¹/₄ fat, 9 g. carbohydrates, 0 cholesterol, 2 g. fat, 2 g. protein, 7 g. fiber, 163 mg. sodium, and 63 calories.
Becky Waggoner

Summer Fruit Pie

2	graham cracker crusts	1	can Mandarin oranges
1	8-oz. pkg. fat-free cream	1	med. can pineapple tidbits
	cheese	1	large tub prepared whipped
1	c. powdered sugar		topping
2	T. milk		

Drain and dice oranges and pineapple and place in pie crust. Fill up with fresh, sliced strawberries. Top with prepared whipped topping, chill and serve.. Makes 2 pies; 8 servings each, 3 g. fat.
Carolyn Moore

Low-Fat Fruit Cocktail Pie

¹/₄	c. lemon juice	1	low-fat graham cracker pie
1	can non-fat condensed milk		crust
1	can fruit cocktail, drained		Fat-free whipped toping
	and rinsed		

Mix lemon juice and milk until smooth. Add fruit. Spoon mixture into crust. Refrigerate until firm, about 2 hours. When ready to serve, top with whipped topping. Serves 8, each 1 g. fat.
Kim McGregor

Bread Pudding

2	eggs	2	T. honey
2	egg whites	1	T. vanilla
1-1/2 c. skim milk		3	slices raisin bread, cubed

Spray 8" round baking dish with non-stick cooking spray. In a large bowl, beat eggs and egg whites until foamy. Beat in milk, honey and vanilla. Stir in bread cubes. Pour into prepared baking dish. Bake in 350 degree oven 35-40 minutes, or until a knife inserted near the center comes out clean. Serves 6, each 128 calories, 3 fat grams.
Donna Foshee

Pumpkin Pudding Cake

2	c. all-purpose flour	1/2	c. canned pumpkin
1/3	c. sugar	1/3	c. vegetable oil
1	tsp baking powder	1	Large egg
1/2	tsp. baking soda	1/2	c. raisins
1/2	tsp. ground cinnamon	1	c. orange juice or water
1/4	tsp. ground cloves	1/2	c. walnuts; chopped

Preheat the oven to 350 degrees. Combine the flour, sugar, baking powder, baking soda, cinnamon and cloves in a bowl. Stir to mix. Add the pumpkin, oil, egg, raisins and orange juice. Beat for 3 minutes. Lightly oil a tube pan. Sprinkle in the nuts. Pour the cake batter over the nuts. Bake for 40 to 50 minutes, until browned. Cool in the pan for 5 minutes before removing. Serve warm with a spoonful of yogurt. Serves 12, each 195 calories, 1 starch, 1 fruit, 1 fat, 3 g. protein, 28 g carbohydrate, 7 g. fat, 62 mg. sodium.
Elizabeth Rodier

Chocolate-Lover's Light Cake

1	pkg. chocolate cake mix	1/2	c. fruit-based fat replacer
1/3	c. unsweetened cocoa powder		(Sunsweet Lighter Bake or
1	4-oz. pkg. instant chocolate		Wonderslim)
	pudding mix	1 1/2	t. vanilla extract
2	c. fat-free sour cream	1	c. mini chocolate chips
1 1/4	c. egg substitute, or 5 egg whites		

Preheat oven to 350 degrees and spray a Bundt pan with canola oil. Combine the cake mix, cocoa powder and pudding mix and mix well. Add sour cream, egg whites, fat replacer and vanilla; mix until blended. Add chocolate chips and stir. Pour into cake pan. Bake 45 to 50 minutes. Cool on rack 20 minutes before removing from pan. Serves 12, each 382 calories, 0 cholesterol, 3 g. fiber, 12 g. fat, 63 g. carbohydrates, 479 mg. sodium.
Diana Prestwood

Mandarin Orange Cake

1	box 2-layer reduced-fat yellow cake mix	3	egg whites
¹/₄	t. baking soda	1	11-oz. can Mandarin orange section with liquid.
1	c. water		

Mix all ingredients. Beat two minutes at medium speed. Bake in three 9-inch pans that have been sprayed with vegetable oil and floured. Bake at 350 degrees for 20-25 minutes. cool completely.

Icing:
15-1/4 oz. can crushed pineapple with juice
9-oz. container low-fat whipped topping
2 small packages sugar-free instant vanilla pudding

Mix pineapple and juice with dry pudding, then add topping and mixed well. Spread between layers; then ice the top and sides of the cake. Refrigerate overnight and serve. Serves 20, each 170 calories, 5 g. fat, 26% fat calories; exchanges: 1¹/₄ starch, ¹/₂ fruit, 1 fat.
Carolyn Moore

Applesauce Cake

¹/₂	c. vegetable oil	1¹/₂	t. salt
2	c. sugar	1	t. cinnamon
2	eggs	¹/₂	t. allspice
1	jar applesauce	¹/₂	c. water
3	c. flour	1¹/₂	c. walnut pieces
1¹/₂	t. baking soda		

With a wire whisk, mix oil, sugar, eggs and applesauce. Add flour, soda and spices; add water. Mix well; add walnuts. Pour into a greased and floured 13 x 9" pan. Bake at 350 for about 45 minutes. Serves 9, each 425 calories; 9 g. fat.
Ofelia M. Alaniz

Lighter Carrot Cake

2	large egg whites	1/2	t. ground cinnamon
1	c. dark brown sugar	1/4	t. ground cloves
1/3	c.canola oil		Pinch ground nutmeg
1/2	c. apple butter	1/2	t. salt
1	t. vanilla extract	2	c. grated carrots
1	c. all-purpose flour, sifted		Canola oil non-stick spray
1	t. baking soda		

Icing:

2	T. soft canola margarine	1 1/2	c. confectioners' sugar,
2	oz. low-fat cream cheese		softened
1	T. grated lemon zest	1/2	t. vanilla
		1	T. skim milk

Prepare one 8-inch layer cake pan with non-stick spray. Combine egg whites, sugar, oil, apple butter, vanilla, and all of the dry ingredients in a bowl and beat until smooth. Stir in the carrots. Pour mixture in the pan. Bake about 30 minutes, or until a toothpick comes out clean in the middle. Turn the cake out onto a wire rack to cool completely. To make icing, beat margarine and cream cheese together until creamy. Mix in the lemon zest, vanilla and sugar. Beat until smooth. Thin with milk if necessary. Cover the cake with the icing and serve immediately. Serves 10, each 333 calories, 11 g. fat, 55 g. carbohydrates, 3 mg. cholesterol, 299 mg. sodium, 3 g. protein.
Jennifer Nguyen

Apple Cake

1	c. white sugar	1	tsp. cinnamon
1	c. brown sugar	1	tsp. allspice
1/2	c. applesauce	3	c. flour
1	tsp baking powder	3	eggs
1	tsp. baking soda	1	c. water
1	tsp salt	3	apples, diced (Granny Smith)
1	tsp. ground cloves		

Mix all together and put into oblong cake pan. Bake at 350 for 45 minutes. Serves 8, only 1 fat gram per serving!
Gale Yost

Hummingbird Cake

3	c. flour	1	c. cooking oil
2	c. sugar	3	large eggs, well beaten
1	tsp ground cinnamon	2	c. chopped banana (3)
1	tsp baking soda	1/2	c. finely chopped walnuts or
1/2	tsp. salt		pecans
1	8 oz can crushed pineapple wit juice	1 1/2	tsp vanilla

Preheat oven to 325 degrees. Generously grease a 10-inch tube or fluted tube pan. In a large mixing bowl, stir together the flour, sugar, cinnamon, baking soda and salt. Remove 2 tablespoons of the juice from the can of pineapple and set aside for the glaze. Add the pineapple, oil, eggs, bananas, nuts and vanilla to the flour mixture. Stir until just blended (do not beat). Pour the batter into the prepared pan. Bake for about an hour and 10 minutes or until a wooden toothpick inserted near the center comes out clean. Cool in the pan, completely. To make the glaze, in a small mixing bowl, combine the melted butter or margarine and the powdered sugar. Add enough of the reserved pineapple juice to make a glaze of drizzling consistency. Drizzle the glaze over the cake. Each slice contains 516 calories and 24 g of fat.

Light Version
Reduce the sugar to 1 3/4 c, substitute 3 tablespoons oil and 1/2 c. applesauce for the oil, reduce to two eggs and reduce the banana to 1 2/3 c. bananas. Each slice now contains 407 calories and 9.5 g. fat.
Helen Raulz

> Earth is here so kind,
> just tickle her with a hoe
> and she laughs with a harvest.
> *Douglas Terrold*

Blackberry Cobbler

3	c. blackberries, fresh or frozen	1¹/₂	c. biscuit mix
³/₄	c. water	¹/₂	c. milk
³/₄	c. sugar	2	T. sugar
2	T. cornstarch mixed with 2 T. water	1	T. butter
			Cinnamon powder

Place blackberries in a pan. Add sugar and water and bring to a boil. Add diluted cornstarch and boil mixture for one minute. Pour into 8 x 8" pan and dot with tiny dabs of butter, then sprinkle with cinnamon. Mix biscuit mix with milk and sugar. Place spoonfuls of mixture on top of berries. Bake at 400 degrees for 20 minutes. Serves 8, each 3 g. fat.
Veronica Laurel

Tropical Delight

1	egg, slightly beaten	16	oz vanilla wafers, crushed
¹/₄	c. margarine	6-8	bananas, cut in slices
¹/₃	c. sugar	1	16-oz can crushed pineapple

Melt margarine in a medium saucepan. Add sugar and mix well. Add pineapple and egg. Mix all ingredients well. Bring to a boil, stirring constantly. Remove from heat and let cool. Cover bottom of an 8 x 8 pan with ¹/₃ of the crushed wafers. Add ¹/₃ of the sliced of bananas. Add ¹/₃ of the pineapple mixture. Repeat twice. Chill for one hour. Serves 8 ; each 325 calories, 4 g. fat.
Zulema L. Cepeda

Mandarin Fruit Salad

1	can Mandarin oranges, drained	1	small tub fat-free whipped topping
1	small can crushed pineapple in juice, drained	1	small box sugar-free orange gelatin.

Mix dry gelatin, whipped topping and pineapple. Fold in oranges. Chill and enjoy! 0 g. fat.
Pat Hall

Guiltless Chocolate Sauce

2   1-oz. squares of unsweetened   2   T. margarine
     chocolate   1   T. vanilla
1   6 oz. can fat-free evaporated   1   T. sugar substitute
     milk

Mix margarine, chocolate and milk in saucepan. Cook and stir over low heat until thick. Remove from heat and add sugar and vanilla. Serve warm over no-sugar added, fat-free ice cream or non-fat yogurt.
Carolyn Moore

Fruit Compote

1   medium can mixed fruit $1/2$ c. cherries, chopped
1   small can pineapple tidbits   1   t. butter
1   banana, chopped

Drain juice from cans of fruit & pour fruit into 8x8 pan. Mix well, spoon a little brown sugar over fruit. Sprinkle cinnamon over all. Dot with butter & heat 30 minutes. Serve s 6, each 45 calories, 1 g. fat.
Dolores Obvenus

Mousse in a Minute

1   small pkg. chocolate instant   1   c. prepared low-fat whipped
      pudding mix   topping
$1^1/2$ c. 2% milk

Prepare pudding mix using $1^1/2$ c. milk. Fold in whipped topping and spoon into dessert dishes. Top with a dollop of topping. Makes 5 servings, each 45 calories, 2g. fat.
Frozen Mousse Pie: Pour mousse into prepared chocolate cookie crumb pie shell and freeze.
Gretchen Grace

Berry Good Recipes!

Banana-Blueberry Sundae

1   banana, peeled and sliced in half lengthwise
3   T. plain nonfat yogurt
1   t. honey
    Handful of blueberries
    Sprinkle of low-fat granola

Mix yogurt with honey and pour over banana. Top with blueberries.
Sprinkle granola over all. Serves one, 35 calories, 0 fat grams.
Anne Messbarger

Blueberry Smoothie Tarts

6   graham cracker single-serve tart crusts
1   pt. fresh blueberries,
1   c. fat-free whipped topping
8   oz. fat-free blueberry yogurt

In a small bowl, blend yogurt and whipped cream. Spoon mixture
into crusts. garnish with strawberries. Chill one hour, or until firm.
Makes 6 tarts, each 2 fat grams.
Maggie McMahon

Pudding Chillers

1	pkg. fat-free instant pudding, any flavor	2	c. cold skim milk
		6	5-oz. paper cups

Pour milk into medium bowl. Add pudding mix. and beat with wire whisk 2 minutes. Spoon into cups. Insert wooden pop sticks into filled cups for a handle. Freeze 5 hours or overnight until firm. To remove pop from cup, place bottom of cup under warm running water for 15 seconds. Press firmly on bottom of cup to release pop. (Do not twist or pull wooden stick…it might break.) Makes 6 pops, each 50 calories, 0 g. fat.
ROCKY ROAD: use chocolate flavor Instant Pudding and stir in $1/2$ cup miniature marshmallows and $1/4$ cup each semi-sweet real chocolate chips and chopped peanuts.
TOFFEE CRUNCH: use vanilla flavor instant pudding and stir in $1/2$ cup chopped chocolate-covered toffee bars.
COOKIES & CREAM: use vanilla flavor instant pudding and stir in $1/2$ cup chopped chocolate sandwich cookies.
Heather Boler

P B & J Wrap

1   8-inch flour tortilla
2 to 3 T. peanut butter

2 to 3 T. grape jelly
1   small banana, peeled

Place tortilla on a paper towel. Microwave 10 to 20 seconds on high until the tortilla is soft and warm. Spread with peanut butter. Top with grape jelly. Place the banana near the right edge of the tortilla. Fold up the bottom fourth of the tortilla. Bring right edge over the banana and roll up. Makes 1 serving.
Maggie Malone

Egg in a Nest

Butter a piece of bread. With a small cup or cookie cutter, cut a hole out of the middle of the bread. Warm a skillet on medium heat. Place bread in skillet, buttered side down. Crack an egg and let the yolk fall into hole of bread. The egg white will spread out over the bread. Let cook for about half a minute. Flip over and cook for another minute or so, until done. Serve with Dippy Soldiers (below). Exchange, 1 medium-fat protein, 1 bread.

Dippy Soldiers

Toast bread, butter it, and cut into 5 strips for dipping into the egg in a nest. Exchange, 1/2 fat, 1 bread.
Philip Beekley

7th Inning Hot Dogs

2   8-oz. cans refrigerated crescent dinner rolls

8   turkey hot dogs, cut in half

Heat oven to 375. Separate dough into 8 rectangles, then cut each rectangle in half to make a triangle. Place a hot dog half lengthwise on 1 end of triangle, then roll up hot dog and press short edges to seal. Place on ungreased cookie sheet. Bake for 11 to 13 minutes or until golden brown. Serve with ketchup, mustard and pickle relish, if desired. Makes 16 servings, each 1 medium-fat meat, 1 bread.
Kim Francis

Cowboy Barbecue Biscuits

10	oz. refrigerated buttermilk biscuits	1	T. cider vinegar
1	lb. ground beef	1/2	tsp. chili powder
1/2	c. ketchup	1	c. (4 oz.) shredded cheddar cheese
3	T. brown sugar		

Separate dough into 10 biscuits; flatten into 5" circles. Press each into the bottom and up the sides of a greased muffin cup; set aside. In a skillet, brown ground beef; drain. In a small bowl, mix ketchup, brown sugar, vinegar and chili powder; stir until smooth. Add to meat and mix well. Divide the meat mixture among biscuit-lined muffin cups, using about 1/4 cup for each. Sprinkle with cheese. Bake at 375 degrees for 18-20 minutes or until golden brown. Cool for 5 minutes before removing from tin and serving. Serves 10 little sandwiches, each 225 calories.
A Volunteer

Baked Macaroni & Cheese

1 1/2	c. macaroni, parboiled 4-5 minutes	1	tsp. salt
2	T. of butter or margarine		pepper to taste
1	tsp. salt		onion powder to taste
2	eggs	2	c. Cheddar cheese, grated
1 1/2	c. milk		optional choice of vegetables (see below)

Ask Mom or Dad to help. Preheat oven to 350. Butter a casserole dish. Place cooked and drained macaroni in the dish. Add butter and salt. Whisk together eggs, milk, salt and spices Pour the beaten milk and egg mixture over the macaroni, making sure the macaroni is "swimming" in the milk. Mix 1 cup grated cheddar cheese into the macaroni/milk mixture. Sprinkle remaining cheese on top. Bake at 350 degrees for 30-45 minutes (until set or golden brown and bubbly). Milk will absorb into the macaroni. Serves 4, each 375 calories, 12 g. fat.
Pat Walker

Make it light! Choose non-fat evaporated milk and low-fat cheese; low-fat olive oil instead of butter. Optional, nutritious (and low-calorie) additions: broccoli florets, chopped spinach, diced red and green bell pepper, baby peas, green beans, carrots, sliced turkey franks, water-pack tuna or chopped chicken.

Fruit Pizza

Sauce:
1/2   c. sugar
2   T. corn starch
Dash salt
3/8   c. water
1/2   c. orange juice
1/8   c. lemon juice
Base:
1   pkg. of prepared sugar cookie dough

Cheese Mixture:
1   8-oz. low-fat cream cheese – softened
1   tsp. vanilla
1/2   c. sugar
Fruit Topping:
Assortment of fresh fruit cut in slices (melon, grapes, strawberries, bananas, berries, etc.)

Prepare the sauce by stirring all ingredients together in a sauce pan and bring to boil over medium heat.. Cook until thick, then chill while preparing the rest of the recipe. Cream together the cheese mixture and set aside. Cut prepared dough into 1/8" thick slices. Lay slices on a greased 12" pizza pan with sides just touching. Bake as directed on cookie dough package. Allow to cool completely. Spread cheese mixture over the cooled cookie crust. Arrange the fruit over the cheese mixture, then pour sauce over the fruit, sealing to the edges (this will keep the bananas from turning dark). Refrigerate until ready to serve. Cut and serve as desired. Exchange, 1 fruit, 2 bread, 1 fat.
Ruth Evins

Cold Veggie Pizza

1   can refrigerated croissant dinner rolls
1   pkg. cream cheese (8 oz.)
1/2   c. sour cream
1   tsp. dill
1/8   tsp. garlic powder

Grated Cheddar or American cheese
Assortment of fresh vegetables cut small or sliced (broccoli, carrots, mushrooms, peppers, etc.)

Separate the dinner roll dough and press evenly unto a pizza pan. Bake at 375 degrees for 8 to 10 minutes to form the pizza crust. Allow to cool completely. In a mixing bowl, blend the cream cheese, sour cream, dill and garlic powder. Spread the cream cheese mixture on the pizza crust. Arrange the vegetables on top of the cream cheese. Sprinkle grated cheese on top as desired and refrigerate until ready to serve. Slice into squares or like traditional pizza. Exchange, 1 bread, 1 vegetable, 1 fat.
Ruth Evins

Low-Calorie Granola

4	c. oatmeal	1/4	tsp. freshly grated nutmeg
1	c. chopped almonds	1/3	c. canola oil
1/4	c. wheat germ	1/2	c. honey
1/2	c. unsalted sunflower seeds	1/2	c. golden raisins
1/4	c. ground flaxseed	1/2	c. grated coconut,
1/2	tsp. cinnamon		unsweetened

In a 4 quart bowl mix oatmeal, almonds, wheat germ and sunflower seeds. Add flaxseed, cinnamon, nutmeg, canola oil and honey. Stir well. Bake on two large cookie sheets at 300 degrees for 25 minutes. Watch carefully so mixture does not burn. Cool. Break up lumps, toast the coconut in oven at 350 degrees for 3 to 5 minutes or until light brown. Return granola to large bowl. Sprinkle with raisins and coconut. Store in sealed jar or airtight bags.
Louise Cisarik

Teddy Bear Sundaes

Any flavor low-fat, fat-free or sugar-free ice cream

M & M's or small candies

Small round chocolate or vanilla wafers

Chocolate sprinkles or toasted coconut

Place a scoop of ice cream on a plate for the head. Use candies for the eyes and mouth. For the ears, push cookies into the ice cream. Sprinkle a little coconut or chocolate sprinkles on top for hair. Calories and fat grams depend on type of ice cream.
Heather Boler

Raspberry Fizz

1¹/₂	c. cranberry-raspberry juice	¹/₂	c. sparkling water
3	scoops raspberry sherbet		

Pour all ingredients into the blender. Cover and blend until the mixture is very smooth. Pour raspberry fizz into glasses and enjoy. Serves 2, each 0 fat grams.
Darrell Hein

Strawberry Smoothie

2	ice cubes	²/₃	c. frozen strawberries
1	c. milk	1¹/₂	tsp. sugar
¹/₃	c. cottage cheese	1	tsp. vanilla extract

Pour all ingredients into a blender. Cover and blend for 45 to 60 seconds until smooth. Pour into glass and enjoy.
Sister Mary Beth

Very Cool Lemonade

6	T. Frozen orange juice concentrate	1	6-oz. can frozen lemonade concentrate
2	T. Frozen grapefruit juice concentrate	1¹/₂	c. cold water Ice cubes

Combine orange juice, grapefruit juice, lemonade and water in a blender. Cover and blend until mixed. Serve over ice if desired. Serves 9, each 0 g. fat; 1 fruit exchange.
Patricia Ward

Peach Paradise Shake

2	10-oz. cans sliced peaches (packed in juice) drained	2	T. orange juice
1²/₃	c. skim milk	2¹/₂	tsp. vanilla flavoring
2¹/₂	T. sugar	10	ice cubes

Place peaches, milk, sugar, orange juice, and vanilla in blender and process until smooth. Add ice, one cube at a time, while processing until mixture is thick. Serve immediately. Serves 4, each 0 g. fat, 1 fruit, 1 low-fat milk.
Christie Galvin

Orange Grape Punch

2	c. water	1/4	c. honey
1	6-oz. can frozen orange juice concentrate	1	12-oz. bottle diet lemon lime carbonated beverage, chilled
1 1/2	c. white grape juice, chilled		
1/4	c. lemon juice		Ice

Combine water and orange juice in a punch bowl; stir to dissolve; stir in white grape juice, lemon juice and honey; Pour carbonated beverage slowly into punch bowl; stir gently to mix. Serve over ice. Serves 12, each 0 g. fat; 1 fruit exchange.
Billy Ward

Purple Fruit Smoothie

2	frozen bananas, peeled and cut into chunks	1	cup orange juice
1/2	c. frozen blueberries	1	T. honey
		1	tsp. vanilla extract

Place bananas, blueberries and juice in a blender, puree. Use honey and/or vanilla to taste. Use more or less liquid depending on the thickness you want for your smoothie. Serves 2, 0 fat grams.
Patricia Ward

Banana Milkshake

1	ripe banana	Dash of nutmeg
1	c. skim milk	

Peel and slice banana. Freeze. After banana is frozen, mix in blender with milk and nutmeg until thick and frosty. Serve immediately. Exchange, 1 fruit.
Laura Thien

Ants on a Log

Celery stalk	Raisins
Peanut butter	

Take a stalk of celery and fill center with peanut butter. Place raisins on top of "log." Enjoy! Serves 1; 1/4 fruit; 1/4 vegetable; 1/4 medium-fat protein.
Melissa Martinez

Apple Cheese Pita

1/4	c. peanut butter	1/4	c. low fat finely shredded
1/4	c. applesauce		cheddar cheese

Stir the above ingredients together. Spread over whole grain bread or pita bread.
Laura Thien

Apple Cheese Spread

3/4	c. peanut butter	1/3	c. low fat finely shredded
1/2	c. applesauce		cheddar cheese

Stir the above ingredients together. Spread over whole grain bread or pita bread.
Laura Thien

Clown Sundae

10	scoops low-fat vanilla ice cream	Red hots
		Chocolate chips
5	sugar cones	Sprinkles

Using an ice cream scoop, stack two round scoops of ice cream in each bowl. Decorate each of the top scoops with red hots, chocolate chips and sprinkles to make a funny face. Put a sugar cone upside-down on top of the top scoop to make a clown hat. Enjoy! Serves 5, each 5-6 g. fat. A fun activity for a birthday party.
A Volunteer

Funny Face Caramel Apples

4	flat 4 inch long wooden sticks	4	medium apples
		1	14-oz. pkg. caramels

Insert sticks into bottom of apples. In 1 quart glass measure, cook unwrapped caramels and 2 tablespoons water on high 3 to 4 minutes until melted, stirring halfway through. Dip apples in caramel, using spoon to coat completely. Place on waxed paper lined plate. Make faces with candy or sprinkles. Freeze 15 minutes. Serve immediately or refrigerate. Makes 4 servings, each 1 fruit, 1 starch.
Melissa Martinez

Banana Chiller

Ripe banana   Wooden pop sticks
Lemon juice   Aluminum foil

Peel and cut bananas in half. Dip in lemon juice. Insert wooden stick in end of banana. Wrap in aluminum foil and freeze. Remove from freezer about 30 minutes before serving. Exchange, 1 fruit.
Laura Thien

Banana Dog

1   banana   Graham cracker crumbs,
2   craft sticks   crushed
     Vanilla fat-free yogurt

Break the banana in half lengthwise and push a craft stick into the flat end of each half. Spread the banana halves with yogurt, then roll them in crumbs. Makes 2 servings, each 0 g fat, 1/2 fruit, 1/4 starch.
Jim Thompson

Alan's Specialty

1   apple   1   slice American cheese, cut
1   T. peanut butter   into strips
                                    Cinnamon

Cut apple into six pieces. Spread peanut butter onto apple pieces. Wrap a strip of cheese around the peanut butter apple. Sprinkle with cinnamon. Enjoy! Exchange, 1 fruit, 1 medium-fat meat, 1 starch.
Al Bordonaro

Paint Sponges

Several small, new kitchen sponges
Cookie cutters in different shapes
Scissors

Place a cookie cutter on top of a sponge and trace the shape with a ballpoint pen. Using scissors carefully, cut out the shape. Dip the sponges in the finger paints to make pretty designs. Try stars, animals, people, circles and triangles.
Grandma Janet

Party Bubbles

1/2	c. water	1 1/2	tsp. white corn syrup
4	T. liquid dish soap		

Blend all ingredients together and pour into a jar or triple the recipe and pour into a large dishpan. Kids will love making giant bubbles with home-made bubble wands. Just slip a 24 inch length of string through a drinking straw; knot the two ends of the string together; dip the straw and string into the bubble solution; lift it up carefully and let the air pass through.
Heather Boler

Grandma's Play Dough

1	c. flour	1	T. oil
1	c. water	2	tsp. cream of tartar
1/2	c. salt	4	drops food coloring

Mix all ingredients in a sauce pan over low heat. Cook until dough pulls from sides of pan. Knead by hand until dough is smooth in texture. Store in tightly closed containers.
Grandma Janet

Finger Paints

1/3	c. cornstarch	2	c. cold water
3	T. sugar		Food coloring

Mix cornstarch, sugar and water in a 1 qt. saucepan. Cook and stir over medium heat about 5 minutes or until thickened; remove from heat. Divide the mixture into separate cups or containers. (Baby food jars work well.) Tint mixture in each container with a different color, using only a few drops of the food coloring. Stir several times until cool. Store in airtight container. Works best if you use the paint the same day you make it. Nontoxic. Try painting with different-shaped, damp sponges for a different effect. Giant art tablets are available in most office supply stores.
Grandma Janet